Our Unprotected Heritage

To the memories of Lynton Keith Caldwell and Robert R. Garvey, Jr. —the geniuses behind NEPA and section 106 of NHPA— this book is respectfully dedicated, with hope for recovering something of their visions.

OUR UNPROTECTED HERITAGE

Whitewashing the Destruction of Our Natural and Cultural Environment

THOMAS F. KING

Left Coast
Press Inc.

WALNUT CREEK, CALIFORNIA

Left Coast Press Inc.

LEFT COAST PRESS, INC.
1630 North Main Street, #400
Walnut Creek, CA 94596
http://www.LCoastPress.com

Copyright © 2009 by Left Coast Press, Inc.

green press INITIATIVE

Left Coast Press is committed to preserving ancient forests and natural resources. We elected to print this title on 30% post consumer recycled paper, processed chlorine free. As a result, for this printing, we have saved:

7 Trees (40' tall and 6-8" diameter)
802 Gallons of Wastewater
2 million BTU's of Total Energy
103 Pounds of Solid Waste
193 Pounds of Greenhouse Gases

Left Coast Press made this paper choice because our printer, Thomson-Shore, Inc., is a member of Green Press Initiative, a nonprofit program dedicated to supporting authors, publishers, and suppliers in their efforts to reduce their use of fiber obtained from endangered forests.

For more information, visit www.greenpressinitiative.org

Environmental impact estimates were made using the Environmental Defense Paper Calculator. For more information visit: www.papercalculator.org.

ISBN 978-1-59874-380-7 hardcover
ISBN 978-1-59874-381-4 paperback

Library of Congress Cataloging-in-Publication Data
Our unprotected heritage : whitewashing the destruction of our cultural and natural environment / Thomas F. King.
   p. cm.— Includes bibliographical references and index.
    ISBN 978-1-59874-380-7 (hbk. : alk. paper)
    ISBN 978-1-59874-381-4 (pbk. : alk. paper)
 1. Cultural property—Protection—United States. 2. Historic preservation—United States. 3. Historic sites—Conservation and restoration—United States. 4. Environmental protection—United States. 5. Nature conservation—United States. 6. Environmental impact analysis—United States. 7. Public interest—United States. 8. Common good. I. Title.
 E159.K565 2009   973—dc22
                2008048712

Printed in the United States of America
∞ The paper used in this publication meets the minimum requirements of American National Standard for Information Sciences—Permanence of Paper for Printed Library Materials, ANSI/NISO Z39.48–1992.

09 10 11 12 13 5 4 3 2 1

CONTENTS

Why This Book?

*D*arkside Development Unlimited wants to build a new shopping mall, sports stadium, speedway, or pig farm in your town or your rural community. The project will devastate some piece of your heritage in the natural or built environment—your neighborhood, or the landscape you love, the family farm, the hill where your tribal elders seek visions, the stream where everybody in your valley goes to fish. Darkside needs some kind of help from the federal government—in other words, from you and me, us taxpayers—to make its project happen. Maybe it needs a federal permit to fill a wetland, or maybe a new access road off the interstate. What can you do to fight the project or seek changes to protect what you treasure?

Realistically, I'm sorry to say, not much—even though there are impressive-sounding federal laws that seem to give your heritage, and everyone's, a degree of protection. I say this based on forty-plus years of increasingly bitter experience with those laws and despite having written half a dozen books encouraging people to use them.

Those laws—the National Environmental Policy Act (NEPA), the National Historic Preservation Act (NHPA), and others—have been around for almost half a century. They say that whenever a federal agency proposes to do something, or proposes to help or permit someone else to do something, that might have impacts on the natural or cultural environment, it has to consider what those impacts are and what it can do to avoid or reduce them. It has to factor them into its planning, consider alternatives, in some cases consult with the interested public about them. Over the decades, most other countries, as well as international organizations like the World Bank, have adopted similar requirements.

As a result, we now have bureaucracies overseeing environmental impact assessment (EIA) and cultural resource management (CRM), and we have well-heeled private companies doing EIA and CRM work under contract. What we do not have is an orderly system for actually, honestly considering and trying to reduce impacts on our natural and cultural heritage. It's all pretty much a sham.

Which is why, when Congress these days decides to do something like build a big fence along our southern border to keep out terrorists, its members don't even blink before waiving EIA and CRM requirements. The notion that these requirements serve an actual purpose—that it's a good idea to think about what damage may result from something you're thinking of doing, before doing it—has been quite lost. Thinking about impacts on the environment is seen as something that's nice to do if you've the time and leisure, but nothing that ought really to influence policy. I've worked in CRM and EIA for over forty years, so I guess I have a vested interest in it, but I find the whole thing rather sad. There *are* good reasons to consider how something we plan may muck up the environment, and to do so before we undertake it. And in a democracy, citizens should have real opportunities to influence what government does, or lets others do, to their heritage. It's too bad, I think, that we've let things develop in such a way that we're spending lots of money on mere public relations efforts, slathering the lipstick of environmental responsibility on the pigs of ill-considered development. We ought to change our system.

So, this book is about what's wrong with environmental impact assessment and its cousin cultural resource management, and what we might do to make them actually work, in the public interest.

ACKNOWLEDGMENTS

No one but I can be accused of having had much to do with the actual writing of this book. However, I'm grateful to Mike Nixon for reviewing the manuscript to alert me to potential legal landmines, and I thank the many colleagues and correspondents who over the years have complained to me about the EIA and CRM systems. They've helped form my own ideas, and I've shamelessly adopted many of their concerns.

I'm also grateful to David Blake of the Buckland Preservation Society, to Nora McDowell and Courtney Coyle of the Fort Mojave Indian Tribe, and to Kathleen Hayden of the Backcountry Horsemen of California, both for ideas and inspiration, and for their comments on those parts of this book that deal with their issues and cases. I thank Ira Beckerman and Richard Galloway for their comments on my blog *précis*, discussed in the afterword, and to John Perkins for comments on the overall manuscript. And as always, I'm thankful to Mitch Allen and his colleagues at Left Coast Press for their encouragement, understanding, and initiative, including Carol Leyba for her skillful and patient editing, and Andrew Brozyna for cover art.

Tom King
Silver Spring, Maryland, USA
November 30, 2008

ONE — Our Unprotected Heritage

Heritage is our legacy from the past, what we live with today, and what we pass on to future generations. Our cultural and natural heritage are both irreplaceable sources of life and inspiration.

UNESCO World Heritage Centre[1]

▪ ▪ ▪ THE MYTH

If you're like most people, there are places in the environment—maybe beautiful natural places, maybe vibrant urban places, maybe places associated with your ancestors—that you think are special and would like to see protected.

If you're like most citizens of the United States, you probably think there are federal laws that protect such places, or at least give them a fighting chance for survival when they're threatened by government action. Perhaps you even think these laws work.

If you've tried to *use* the laws to protect some piece of your own natural or cultural heritage—your neighborhood, your family farm, the stream where your family's always fished—you probably know better. You know how ineffective the laws really are, and how frustrating it is to try, and usually fail, to make them work.

You know that when you're up against forces of development—whether it's the U.S. government, a state highway department, a sprawl developer, or a big box store—you're likely to find that people in authority discriminate against the environment that's precious to you. What's important to you may not even be noticed unless you not only make a huge fuss, but use just the right words in doing so, push just the right bureaucratic buttons, at just the right times. If it *is* noticed, it may not be enough that it's precious to you and perhaps all your neighbors or the members of your community. If the place you want to save doesn't impress a professional of some kind, and meet narrowly defined and hard-to-understand technical criteria, it's likely to be given very short shrift.

If you've tried to use the laws, you know that strange and esoteric administrative systems have been developed to "implement" them and that the procedures for using them can be impenetrable to an ordinary citizen, however smart and educated that citizen may be.

And you know that even if you learn the systems, learn to use the specialized language and push the right buttons, at the end of the day you're still likely to see government agencies agree, over your head, to let your heritage go down the drain.

If you *haven't* tried to use the laws, it may surprise you to learn that such problems exist. After all, you read and hear all the time about environmental impact statements being prepared; about animals and plants being placed (or not placed) on lists of threatened and endangered species. You read and hear about regulatory agencies fighting over what a highway or a surface mine will do to the environment, or whether it's OK to knock down an old building or bulldoze an archaeological site. All those things do happen, and they reflect the workings of large bureaucracies and much larger professional consulting industries that do "environmental impact assessment" (EIA) and "cultural resource management" (CRM). But if you get entangled in the EIA or CRM games yourself, I'm afraid you'll be in for a rude awakening.

For over forty years, I've worked with the laws that ostensibly protect the human environment from thoughtless destruction. I helped create some of the regulatory systems they mandate; I know the language and how the systems work. Over that time—especially in the last decade or so—I've become more and more dismayed at what we've created. I think it's time—and past time—for some serious changes to be made.

■ ■ ■ "ENVIRONMENT" AND "HERITAGE"

The laws that are supposed to protect aspects of the environment are all casually called "environmental" laws. It's important to understand, though, that there are two quite different kinds of environmental laws in the United States. An insightful study prepared back in 1992 for the U.S. Army[2] described them as representing "two shades of green." On the one hand are what might be called "bright green" environmental laws;[3] on the other are "light green" laws.[4]

Bright Green Laws

The bright green laws contain more or less rigid standards and external enforcement systems; the parents of them all (not in age, but in the sense of being role models) are the Resource Conservation and Recovery Act (RCRA) of 1976 and the Comprehensive Environmental Response, Compensation, and Liability Act (CERCLA) of 1980—the so-called Superfund law. Under RCRA and CERCLA, if you toxify the environment—dump some awful chemical into the water or on the ground—and you get caught by an enforcement agency—generally the U.S. Environmental Protection Agency or one of its state equivalents—you're going to pay, big-time, to clean up the mess . . . unless you find a way to squirm out of it. Another bright green law is the Clean Air Act, which sets definite standards for air quality that are not supposed to be exceeded by those who (individually or collectively) pump gunk into the atmosphere. Elements of the Clean Water Act also fall into the bright green category. What distinguishes the bright green laws is that:

a They apply more or less to everybody.

b They involve more or less hard-and-fast quantitative criteria— thou shall not pump more than N parts per million of Ugly Chemical X into the environment.

c They give enforcement authority to some agency, which can, if it finds you've violated one of the laws, make you pay serious money and in some cases send you to jail.

   d   They have created government and non-governmental programs managed mostly by environmental engineers—who often think the bright green laws are the *only* environmental laws that really matter.

Light Green Laws

The "light green" laws are different, softer, more loosey-goosey. Two of the key light green laws are the National Environmental Policy Act (NEPA)—which has created the EIA business—and the National Historic Preservation Act (NHPA), which has produced CRM. These laws have the following characteristics that separate them from their bright green brethren.

   a   They apply mostly to federal agencies—in many ways they're designed to protect us, the public, *from* our government.

   b   They involve soft, more or less subjective criteria and standards and really don't prohibit anything very specific; they require only that government's effects on the environment be *considered*, thought about, and—in theory—dealt with in some responsible way.

   c   Violating them almost never results in a fine or a jail term.

   d   They're supposed to be self-enforcing—that is, federal agencies are supposed to police themselves and do right by the laws—with oversight by the courts, of course.

   e   The programs that—in theory—make them work are administered by natural and social scientists—biologists, ecologists, geologists, archaeologists, historians, and the like.

A few laws, like the Endangered Species Act (ESA), straddle the boundary between bright and light, containing elements of each.

This book is mostly about the "light green" laws, which are the ones most often used by people trying to save aspects of their natural and cultural heritage. Since the engineers who dominate practice under the "bright green" laws have made the word "environment" their own, I have to use another term for the light greenies, so I call them the "heritage laws." A rather precious name, but not inaccurate; they're the laws that are supposed to protect our natural and cultural heritage in the environment—the places and things that we citizens cherish—from thoughtless desecration.

I focus on the heritage laws not because I think the bright green laws are working fine; I doubt very much if they are. It's just that I specialize in the light green laws, and there's quite enough wrong with *them* to fill this book.

■ ■ ■ FORTY YEARS WITH THE HERITAGE LAWS

In 1966, Congress passed a law called the National Historic Preservation Act (NHPA). One of the law's major purposes was to get federal agencies—the Federal Highway Administration, for example, the Army Corps of Engineers, and the then-shiny-new Department of Housing and Urban Development—to stop thoughtlessly destroying the nation's historic buildings, sites, landscapes, and neighborhoods. Three years later came the National Environmental Policy Act (NEPA), designed to make such agencies more careful about the whole human environment. About three years after that, Congress enacted the Endangered Species Act (ESA); in the meantime it passed laws designed to protect the quality of water (the Clean Water Act, 1972) and air (the Clean Air Act, 1970).

NEPA and NHPA are the major federal heritage laws this book is about, though I'll touch on the others from time to time.[5]

Over the forty years since NEPA and NHPA came into being, a multibillion-dollar industry has grown up dedicated to helping federal agencies—and non-federal developers who need federal assistance or permits—do what the laws require. A considerable federal-state bureaucracy has developed to oversee compliance with them. Environmental impact assessment (EIA) and what's widely if inaccurately called "cultural resource management" (CRM) have become routine parts of federal, state, local, and regulated private development planning.[6]

At the same time, we've drifted away from the intent of the laws, making them more and more pointless, less and less useful in protecting anything, except the profit margins of some companies and the jobs of some government employees. Today,

◈ The average study of a proposed project's impacts on the cultural or natural environment is done by consultants employed by that very project's proponent, who can fire them if they don't give his project a clean bill of health.

◈ The federal and state agencies responsible for overseeing the studies and keeping them honest usually view themselves—though they'll seldom admit it—as being in the business of making sure projects go forward with as little impediment as possible from the environment. Or they're mostly concerned with processing paperwork and protecting themselves, or they've turned into petty tyrants, intent on making sure that things are done the way they want them done, with all the forms filled out the way they want them filled out.

◈ And the systems for compliance with the laws have become so esoteric, so laden with jargon and obscure procedures, that citizens— whose heritage the laws are intended to protect—have little chance to get their concerns heard, their heritage taken care of, or even to understand what is and isn't being done to "protect the environment." Few real opportunities exist to negotiate with project proponents for the protection of your heritage.

This book is about what's happened to transform the bright hopes of the heritage laws into dull, pointless exercises in futility and frustration— for everyone but some bureaucrats whose jobs and status depend on the system, many consultants who know how to play the system to make money, and a few academics who are able to make the system support their research interests. And it's about what we can do to change things, if we're interested in holding onto some vestiges of our heritage for our grandchildren.

I'll give considerable attention to what happens in "compliance" with section 106 of NHPA, which says that agencies have to consider the effects of their actions and decisions on historic places. I've spent much of my life working in the section 106 compliance game, and I know rather intimately what's happened to it. And in theory, I think, the project review process under section 106 ought to be a model for review under all the laws—focusing as it does (again theoretically) on open-minded *consultation* among diverse parties to reach compromises between development and preservation. Section 106 review has long since stopped even coming close to achieving its purposes—or any purpose, for that matter—and the same goes for NEPA. The systems designed back in the 1970s to make the heritage laws work have become deeply corrupted. It's time to do something about them.

■ ■ ■ NOTHING NEW

This book does not plow very new ground. Other books, journal articles, and web pages have critiqued the government's compliance with NEPA and, to a lesser extent, with NHPA. Notable among the former are two books, one by the late Lynton Keith Caldwell from 1998[7] and the other by Matthew Lindstrom and Zachary Smith from 2001.[8] Frank Fischer has written eloquently and at length about the lack of public access to NEPA and similar laws[9]—one of my major complaints. But Caldwell, Lindstrom, Smith and Fischer have all written about the laws—mostly NEPA—from a more or less academic perspective, emphasizing matters of policy and politics. My perspective is that of a laborer in the NEPA and NHPA vineyards, critiquing the EIA and CRM systems from the inside. In articulating this perspective, I hope I can add something to the discussion. In Chapter Eight I'll return to the works of Caldwell and others in musing about what might be done to make the NEPA and NHPA review systems actually work in the way Congress intended them to.

■ ■ ■ JUST TO BE CLEAR: PRESERVATION VERSUS CONSIDERATION

I should make it clear at the outset that NEPA and NHPA do not—and, in my very strong opinion, *should* not—mandate that heritage be preserved at the expense of meeting contemporary needs or respecting individual rights. Some local laws do that—for instance, some (but not all)

15

local historic landmark laws prescribe what colors homeowners can paint their homes and proscribe doing anything that changes the character of a designated historic district. But what the federal heritage laws call for is much more modest and flexible: that protection of heritage be *fairly considered* in planning modern actions. Sometimes that consideration will lead to full-scale protection, sometimes to full-scale destruction. Most often it should produce some sort of compromise designed—well or poorly—to meet the purposes and needs of the modern world while doing something to avoid totally wasting the environment. Unless we're ready to stop doing everything else civilization insists on doing—growing crops, launching expeditions into space, fighting wars, moving people and goods from one place to another—such compromises are necessary and the best we can expect or demand on behalf of our heritage. But we ought to be able to expect honest efforts to reach such compromises, and that, regrettably, we can't presently do.

■ ■ ■ THE LAWS

So what are the heritage laws, and what are they designed to do? This won't be a comprehensive review—just enough to give us a basis for examining how poorly they do it.

Sections 101 and 102(2)(c) of NEPA

The National Environmental Policy Act (NEPA) came into being at the very end of the 1960s. The policy promised in its title is laid out in section 101. The U.S. government, it says, will "use all practicable means and measures" to "create and maintain conditions under which man and nature can exist in productive harmony." Government will be a "trustee of the environment for succeeding generations." It will "assure . . . safe, healthful, productive, and esthetically and culturally pleasing surroundings." It will use the environment "without degradation," "preserve important historic, cultural and natural aspects of our national heritage," and support "diversity and variety of individual choice."

But agencies and the courts have paid little real attention to section 101; NEPA is understood to be a "procedural law," based on section 102(2)(c). Section 102(2)(c) is the action-forcing part of the law. It says that federal agencies must prepare "detailed statements" describing the environmental impacts of

◈ things an agency does itself (such as manage public land, run military bases);

◈ things an agency helps someone else do (federal assistance to high-way construction, for instance); and

◈ things an agency permits someone else to do (for example, dumping fill in a waterway or wetland, which requires a Clean Water Act permit from the Army Corps of Engineers).

Agencies have to prepare such "statements" *if* their actions may "significantly affect the quality of the human environment."

These statements are called "environmental impact statements" (EIS). They become part of the record the agency and others consider in deciding whether and how to proceed with their projects. Regulations[10] issued by the Council on Environmental Quality—part of the Executive Office of the President—specify how EISs are to be prepared, reviewed by the public, finalized, and used.

The regulations also guide agencies in figuring out whether a proposed action may have significant effects and hence require an EIS. This involves completing a study called an "environmental assessment" (EA). Concerned parties—like you—should have opportunities to influence agencies in deciding (a) whether an impact is significant and (b) what to do about it. Public involvement in NEPA review, however—particularly in the development of EAs—is not very thoroughly, clearly, or creatively provided for in the regulations. As we'll see, this is part of a larger problem; the impermeability of NEPA review to the public is, I think, one of the main reasons the promises of section 101 haven't been fulfilled.

Section 106 of NHPA

The National Historic Preservation Act (NHPA) was enacted in 1966 as part of the initiative spearheaded by Lady Bird Johnson to promote the beautification of America. Amended often since then, NHPA has many parts, but the key provision for purposes of saving pieces of heritage from destruction is section 106. Section 106 says that federal agencies must "take into account"—that is, consider—the effects of their actions on "historic properties."

The types of actions that must be reviewed under section 106 are the same types that have to be considered under NEPA—things a federal agency does, helps someone else do, or permits someone else to do. The "historic properties" on which agencies are to take effects into account are those included in—or, very importantly, *not* included in but simply *eligible for*—the "National Register of Historic Places." The Register is kept by the National Park Service, but the places it lists are all over the place—on federal, state, local, Indian tribal, and private land.

In theory, agencies comply with section 106 by following regulations[11] issued by the Advisory Council on Historic Preservation, an independent federal oversight and rulemaking body. "Independent" means it's not part of an executive department like the Department of the Interior; it reports directly to the president and Congress. The regulations prescribe a rather intricate process of project review that features consultation with state and local government and other interested parties—like you and me, in theory—to identify historic properties and decide how to minimize impacts on them. The consultation is supposed to be open to anyone who's got concerns about a project's effects on historic places, and it's supposed to result in binding agreements about whether and how to proceed with whatever action the government is considering.

Other Light Green Laws and Executive Orders Related to NEPA

As I've mentioned, NEPA and section 106 aren't the only "light green" EIA laws. NEPA is often referred to as an "umbrella" under which other laws huddle. There are many laws and executive orders—presidential directions to the agencies—that crowd under the NEPA bumbershoot. Each of these laws is independent and deals with some particular kind of environmental resource or situation, but they all relate in practical ways to NEPA and sometimes to section 106 of NHPA. There is no point in going into these in detail, but here are some examples.

The Endangered Species Act (ESA)

Just as NHPA focuses on "historic properties" listed in or eligible for a national register, the ESA focuses on lists of endangered and threatened species. These lists are administered by the Fish and Wildlife Service (FWS), a part of the Department of the Interior, though Fish and Wildlife shares the responsibility to actually list species with the National Marine Fisheries Service (NMF) in the National Oceanic and Atmospheric Administration, part of the Department of Commerce. These agencies not only list endangered and threatened species, but also outline the "critical habitats" of each. Federal agencies are required to consult with FWS and/or NMF (depending on the species involved) before doing, assisting, or permitting anything that might damage an endangered or threatened species or its critical habitat. No one, in or out of government, is supposed to "take" an endangered species without permission from FWS or NMF, and there are rather elaborate regulations for obtaining such permission under different circumstances. In most cases, it is possible to take or otherwise affect members of a threatened or endangered species after due consideration of alternatives and of ways to mitigate the damage.[12]

Section 404 of the Clean Water Act

This law prohibits filling a wetland without the permission of the Corps of Engineers. It's a bright green law in that it applies to everyone, it requires an actual permit, and you can be fined for violating it. It's lighter green in that it allows the Corps to exercise its judgment, rather than apply hard, quantitative standards. The Corps has to consider *not* issuing a permit, and it has to look at alternatives and mitigation measures—notably measures that will compensate for wetlands lost—but it is very rare for a permit to be denied.[13]

Executive Order 11988

This executive order discourages development on floodplains. Executive orders aren't laws; they're directions from the president to the executive branch that build on and interpret existing law. This executive order, among other provisions, requires that agencies examine the impacts of their actions on floodplains as part of their NEPA analyses and give precedence to alternatives that avoid or minimize floodplain effects.[14]

The Religious Freedom Restoration Act (RFRA) and the American Indian Religious Freedom Act (AIRFA)

I think of these laws as heritage laws because—besides the fact that religion is part of most people's heritage—they cause agencies to think about the effects of their actions on religious practices and beliefs. Or they should. AIRFA guarantees American Indians the right to free exercise of their traditional religions. RFRA says that government will not unduly burden the practice of anyone's religion unless there's a compelling government interest in doing so. So in carrying out EIA, or doing CRM, it's necessary—in theory—to consider the religious values that people may ascribe to aspects of the environment and try to minimize impacts on them.[15]

Executive Order 12898: Environmental Justice

This executive order tells federal agencies to avoid disproportionate and adverse environmental effects on low-income people and minority groups. While it's mostly thought of as a pollution prevention requirement—don't pollute the poor or minority neighborhood—it relates to all kinds of impacts on all aspects of the environment. So—in theory, as always—it gives minority and low-income groups a little more power than they would otherwise have in insisting that agencies consider effects on their heritage, whatever that heritage may be.[16]

■ ■ ■ WHAT THE HERITAGE LAWS DO AND DON'T DO

Section 106 of NHPA requires agencies to think and consult about their impacts on historic places, and reduce, avoid, or minimize them where feasible. NEPA requires an examination of potential impacts on the whole environment. The courts have specified that in performing such review, agencies are supposed to take a "hard look" at the damage their actions may cause and at alternatives that may avoid, reduce, or somehow make up for that damage. The idea is to get agencies to look before they leap— figure out what will be messed up if they do what they're thinking about doing, and see what can be done to minimize harm or even avoid it altogether. In many cases, the agency may in the end decide to take the action despite the destruction it causes, but—in theory as usual—if everyone works at it in good faith, less damaging alternatives can be found.

But . . .

That's the theory, and back in the 1970s when the EIA and CRM enterprises were getting underway, we had high hopes they would make federal decision making responsive to public interests in our collective heritage. Unfortunately, what's worked out has been pretty disappointing. One federal court's observation on a section 106 case pretty well sums up standard practice under both NHPA and NEPA:

> NHPA requires an agency to "stop, look, and listen," (but) in the present case. . . [d]efendants merely paused, glanced, and turned a deaf ear.[17]

A good deal of what's gone bad in the last eight years results from the Bush administration's scorn for environmental protection, federal regulation, and anyone who doesn't own a lot of stock in petroleum companies. Environmental budgets have been cut, proponents of vigorous environmental compliance have been eased or forced out of government or into assignments where they can't be heard or seen, and oversight agencies have been strongly encouraged to divert their attention to concerns other than compliance.[18] The Council on Environmental Quality in 2003 proposed a number of milquetoast actions to "modernize" NEPA and has spent the last five years digesting its own report.[19] The Advisory Council on Historic Preservation, which theoretically oversees section 106 review, has devoted itself to awarding "Preserve America" grants.[20] The Fish and Wildlife Service, after much fretting, finally managed to list the polar bear as a threatened species under the Endangered Species Act, but under political pressure couldn't draw the obvious linkages between that species' plight and what humans are doing to melt its habitat out from under it. The action agencies—the Corps of Engineers, Bureau of Land Management, Department of Housing and Urban Development, and all the others—have taken their cues from the White House and become less and less sensitive to what the public thinks of them, less and less concerned about the intent of the laws. Without leadership or responsible policy, the practice of assessing impacts on heritage has become a rote exercise of "clearing"—that is, rubber-stamping—development plans. In many cases, the practice has become blatantly corrupt; in most if not all others, it simply doesn't work. And the only reform anyone seems to consider involves "stream-lining" compliance to make it even less meaningful than it is now.

But the corruption hasn't resulted only from what the Bush administration has and hasn't done. There's more—and in a way less—to it than that. The heritage laws, or at least the regulatory systems that supposedly implement them, are fundamentally flawed; they weren't very realistically thought through at the outset, and over the decades they've evolved in some very strange directions. This was happening before George W. Bush ever thought about the White House; his administration has simply brought things to a head.

It comes down to this: The laws—particularly NEPA and NHPA—not only put foxes in charge of guarding the henhouse; they charge them with designing and monitoring the security systems.

We should have recognized from the start that this couldn't work, but we didn't, or didn't want to. Today we're living with the results, and sadly, most of us—practitioners of the heritage laws, that is—are satisfied with them. Or we're so used to them that we can envision nothing else.

■ ■ ■ MY EXAMPLES

It's easiest to illustrate what's wrong by using examples. Here are some cases that will weave their way through the rest of this book; I'll touch on others as needed.

Abó Pass, New Mexico

Abó Pass connects the Rio Grande Valley on the west and the Salinas area on the east, about an hour's drive south of Albuquerque. It's quite an obvious break in the mountains east of the Rio Grande, with the Manzano Mountains to the north and Los Pinos Mountains to the south. It's drained by an extensive system of arroyos flowing into a central stream, Abó Canyon. Most of the land is private ranchland, though Abó Mission, one unit of the National Park Service's Salinas Pueblo Missions National Monument, lies at the head of the pass. Abó Canyon drains the pass into the Rio Grande; it's a perennial stream with many tributaries—a major water source in this arid country.

Back in the early days of the twentieth century, the Santa Fe Railroad built a line through the canyon. Santa Fe's successor, Burlington Northern-Santa Fe (BNSF), runs the line today, and a few years ago announced plans for a second track roughly parallel to the first but involving large new cuts and fills through about three miles of canyon country, to speed traffic through to the east and west. The track would cross some federal land and fill some wetlands regulated by the U.S. Army Corps of Engineers, so it got reviewed under NEPA and section 106 of NHPA.

Ranchers in the pass weren't very happy about the new railroad chewing up the landscape and interfering with their cattle, but most didn't think they could fight BNSF. The owners of Dripping Springs Ranch—Luis Rosas and his wife, Jean Sawyer-Rosas—decided to try, deploying section 106 of NHPA as one of their weapons.[21]

Buckland, Virginia

Buckland is a little eighteenth-century mill village on Broad Run in northern Virginia. It's also the site of the Battle of Buckland Mills during the Civil War—where, to simplify a bit, J. E. B. Stuart sent George Armstrong Custer fleeing in what's sometimes referred to as "Custer's First Stand." Today it's on the leading edge of the suburban sprawl that has metastasized from Washington, DC. Tract housing and strip malls are creeping steadily closer to the edge of the battlefield and the east bank of Broad Run; Buckland lies on the west bank.

A group of local residents, organized as the Buckland Preservation Society, is trying to save the village and its surrounding agricultural landscapes.[22] Many planned construction projects in the area—roads, housing developments, and the like—either involve federal funding or require federal permits to fill wetlands, so they have to be reviewed under NEPA and section 106.

The Topock Maze Landscape, California and Arizona

On the high desert just west of the Colorado River near Needles, California, the Topock (or Mystic) Maze is a complex of windrows raked in the desert pavement.[23] In the traditions of the Mojave Tribe, the Maze and other parts of the local landscape make up the entrance to the spirit world; the dead must pass through the Maze to its spiritual twin on "the other side."[24] Unfortunately, the Maze landscape lies athwart some other pathways, too—old Route 66, modern Interstate 40, a BNSF rail line, and a pipeline maintained by Pacific Gas and Electric Company (PG&E).

Fans of the film "Erin Brockovich" will remember PG&E from its hexavalent chromium dumping, whose impacts on a small community's health plunged Ms. Brockovich into her career as a toxic-waste fighter. It hasn't been made into a movie yet, but the company dumped hexavalent chromium in an arroyo that runs across the Topock Maze too, and a plume of the stuff has been working its way down toward the river. The U.S. Department of the Interior's Bureau of Land Management (BLM), which controls much of the land in the area, is working with PG&E and the state toxic waste agencies in California and Arizona to clean up the plume, which involves lots of well-drilling, pumping, and trucking toxic stuff hither and thither. The Fort Mojave Indian Tribe, whose reservation lies nearby, has tried to use section 106 of NHPA to protect the cultural and religious character of the area's landscape from the disruption the cleanup entails—without impeding the cleanup itself.

In the interests of full disclosure, I have to acknowledge that the Rosas, the Buckland Preservation Society, and the Fort Mojave Tribe have all hired me at one time or another to help them protect their interests under NHPA and NEPA. This is why I've gotten enough experience with the cases to be able to write about them. But the "other side"—BNSF, PG&E, development interests in Virginia—have far more and pricier consultants helping them. And one thing that's dawned on me as I've worked with Abó Canyon, Buckland, and the Topock Maze is that they're just the tip of a large and mostly invisible iceberg. The people involved in these cases—my clients—are among the very rare ordinary citizens who can afford to retain services like mine, even at discounted rates. For every one of them there are scores, hundreds, probably thousands of other groups that remain largely unrepresented, without assistance in trying, however fruitlessly, to make the heritage protection systems work for them. I hear from some of these people, and I try to help them if I can.

I hear from the "Between the Rivers" families, descendants of Revolutionary War soldiers who got thrown off their ancestral lands between the Cumberland and Tennessee Rivers in western Kentucky and Tennessee when the river valleys were flooded by the Tennessee Valley Authority (TVA). Their land was turned into Land Between the Lakes National Recreation Area.[25] Land Between the Lakes is administered by the Forest Service, and the Between the Rivers people would like to help the government manage the area so their cultural connections with it won't be lost. They've tried to use section 106 of NHPA to persuade the Forest Service to consult with them but have been stiffed by the government.

I hear from Geoffrey Sea, a property owner and writer in Ohio who's trying to protect his historic farmstead and a complex of ancient Hopewell mounds from the impacts of a nuclear fuel reprocessing facility on adjacent land controlled by the Department of Energy. Geoffrey's been trying to get the Department and the Nuclear Regulatory Commission to listen to him as they "comply" with NHPA and NEPA, but they've shut him out.[26]

I hear from Kathleen Hayden and the Backcountry Horsemen of California, who are trying to keep wild horse herds alive as part of the heritage of the American West, struggling against federal and state land management agencies that seem to be "managing" them out of existence.[27]

I hear from the residents of Duncan's Point, a small African-American community on the shores of Lake of the Ozarks in Missouri,[28] who are trying to keep their historic park from being messed up by a federally regulated sewage treatment plant, and from the people of Benton Harbor on Lake Michigan, who are trying to keep a golf course out of their much-prized Jean Klock Park.[29]

I hear from—and worked for awhile with—the Indian tribes along the Klamath River who want the Federal Energy Regulatory Commission (FERC) to factor the cultural value of the river's salmon runs into its decisions about removing hydroelectric dams that impede the fish migration.[30] I hear from Indians and Native Hawaiians trying to get the National Science Foundation (NSF) and National Aeronautics and Space Administration (NASA) to consult with them before deciding whether and how to build astronomical telescopes on the tops of mountains they regard as spiritual places.[31]

The list goes on and on. I try to advise people like these when they call up or send me emails, but I can't do very much without getting paid, and they usually can't afford to pay me. The agencies and companies they're struggling with, however, *can* afford to pay people like me to help them advance *their* interests. I'm not saying that all the people who come to me with their problems ought to prevail, but I'm enough of a populist to think that they ought to be *heard*, and negotiated with in good faith, and that they ought to have a level playing field on which to contend. They aren't and they don't, and in a democracy, that strikes me as a problem.

■ ■ ■ PIECES OF THE PUZZLE

The failure of the heritage laws has several aspects, several parts, that interact with and reinforce one another. These are:

◈ The analyst as proponent: The people analyzing a project's impacts on the natural and cultural environment act as agents for the project's sponsors.

◈ Reviewers as advocates: The government agencies assigned review and oversight functions by the laws have become, in effect, advocates for the proposals whose merits and weaknesses they are supposed to judge.

◈ Undue complexity: Review systems have become so complicated and burdened with esoteric language and procedures that no one but specialists can understand them.

◈ Petty dictators and absent overseers: Oversight and review agencies seek to advance their own agendas, build their own power, or simply avoid controversy and survive, rather than making the laws work for the public whose interests they're supposed to represent.

◈ Pro-forma "public comment" and "public hearings" are substituted for meaningful consultation with concerned parties.

◈ Agencies and project planners are disinclined ever to rethink their plans in response to public objections, and are inclined, as a result, to find ways to reject and bury such concerns, even if it requires twisting or ignoring facts.

In the next few chapters we'll look at each of these problem areas and how they interact with one another.

WHAT'S SUPPOSED TO HAPPEN: NEPA

What regulations are followed?

The regulations of the Council on Environmental Quality *(CEQ)* for implementing the procedural provisions of NEPA—codified at *40 CFR 1500 through 1508*, and agency-specific NEPA regulations.

What gets reviewed?

Everything a federal agency plans to do, helps someone else do, or permits someone else to do, except types of action the agency *categorically excludes* because they have (in theory) little or no potential for significant environmental impact. Also actions that ordinarily *are* categorically excluded, where the agency finds that *extraordinary circumstances* require further study.

How does it work?

1   The federal agency determines whether the action may have a *"significant impact on the quality of the human environment."* This may be obvious, or it may require studies of various kinds, which collectively are referred to as making up an *environmental assessment (EA)*.

2   The agency either:

   a   issues a *finding of no significant impact (FONSI)* in which it asserts that the action will have no significant impact on the quality of the human environment, or

   b   undertakes an *environmental impact statement (EIS)*.

3   If an EIS is to be prepared, the agency:

   a   publishes a *notice of intent (NOI)* to do so;

   b   undertakes *scoping* to decide what the scope of analysis will be;

   c   carries out the studies it has decided make up the scope;

   d   issues a *draft EIS (DEIS)* for review and comment by other government agencies, organizations, and the public;

   e   responds to comments, which may involve changes to the EIS and/or doing further studies, consultations, and analyses; and

   f   issues a *final EIS (FEIS)*.

4   The agency's (and other) decision makers consider the results and findings of the EIS in deciding whether and how to carry out, assist, or permit the action.

5   Once a decision is made, the agency publishes a *record of decision (ROD)*.

6   The agency (and/or others with the agency's blessing) carries out the decision.

There are quite a few textbooks that provide detail about NEPA requirements, most of them focusing largely on the preparation of EISs. Several are listed under "Sources" at the end of this book.[32]

What's Supposed to Happen: Section 106 of NHPA

What regulations are followed?

The regulations of the *Advisory Council on Historic Preservation (ACHP)*, codified at 36 CFR 800.

What gets reviewed?

Anything a federal agency plans to do, helps someone else do, or permits someone else to do, provided it represents a type of action with the potential to affect historic properties—that is, places included in or eligible for the National Register of Historic Places. This doesn't mean that the agency needs to know there are historic properties to be affected, only that the action be the kind of thing that in theory can affect them—through demolition, earth moving, changes in land use, and the like.

How does it work?

1 The federal agency initiates consultation with the State and/or Tribal Historic Preservation Officer (SHPO/THPO), Indian tribes, and (in theory) others interested in the action (called an *undertaking*) and its possible effects on known or unknown historic properties; these people are called *consulting parties*.

2 With the consulting parties, the agency determines the *scope* of what it needs to do to find historic properties and determine how they may be affected. One important part of scoping is determining the *area of potential effects (APE)*—the area where the undertaking may affect historic properties.

3 The agency undertakes *identification* of historic places and effects within the APE, usually involving surveys and other kinds of studies, in consultation with the consulting parties.

4 The agency determines whether places in the APE are *eligible for the National Register of Historic Places,* following National Park Service (NPS) regulations, in consultation with the SHPO/THPO and (in theory) other consulting parties.

5 The agency determines whether the proposed action will have *adverse effects* on historic properties, using criteria in the Advisory Council on Historic Preservation (ACHP) regulations. If not, it proposes a *determination of no adverse effect* for concurrence by the SHPO/THPO and other consulting parties.

6 If there will be an *adverse effect,* or if the SHPO or THPO doesn't agree with a determination of no adverse effect, the consulting parties consult to find ways to *resolve* the adverse effect. This usually leads to a *memorandum of agreement (MOA),* whose terms the agency ensures are carried out.

7 If an MOA isn't reached, the ACHP *comments* to the head of the federal agency, who *considers the comments* in deciding

whether and how to carry out or approve the action, but need not follow them.

Textbooks on section 106, other parts of NHPA, and related legal authorities are considerably rarer than textbooks on NEPA practice. Several are listed at the end of this book under "Sources," however.[33]

Two
The Analyst as Proponent

Agencies shall insure the professional integrity, including scientific integrity, of the discussions and analyses in environmental impact statements.

Council on Environmental Quality:
NEPA regulations at 40 CFR 1502.24

At the annual conference of the National Association of Environmental Professionals (NAEP)[1] a couple of years ago, I walked into the exhibit hall where many environmental impact assessment (EIA) and cultural resource management (CRM) firms had displays touting their services. The first thing I saw was a huge image of the earth from the moon, hanging over the exhibit of a major firm that does both EIA and CRM work. The very professional-looking caption, in about 300-point characters, read:

"Your project means the world to us!"

The sign disoriented me, and after a few moments staring at it I realized why. The slogan was undoubtedly true and applied to every company in the room. EIA and CRM firms survive from project to project. They wouldn't exist if they didn't get hired to evaluate the impacts of projects, and to develop ways to avoid, reduce, or otherwise mitigate them. And the people who hire them, for the most part, are project proponents. So a proponent's project really does mean "the world"—that is, survival—to an EIA or CRM firm.

But the sentiment was—is—all wrong. Not for the project proponent, who certainly ought to be bullish about his or her project, but for the people who are supposed to weigh and balance and accurately describe its impacts on the environment. If we're so enthusiastic about our client's project, how can we possibly do a responsible, even semi-objective job of analyzing its impacts? Particularly since, if we're working at their pleasure, we have to keep our clients reasonably happy with us. The client wants to build his project, that's understandable, and if we seem to be throwing up environmental roadblocks, he's probably going to start shopping for another consultant.

This seems pretty obvious; my epiphany didn't require a lot of brainpower. But what struck me was this: *no one else at the conference seemed bothered by it.*

This is probably because we're all used to it. Most EIA work in this country, and most CRM studies, are done by companies working on behalf of project proponents. Most people who work for such companies, and who run them, have spent most or all their professional lives working within this system. Advancing our clients' interests, acting as part of our clients' planning teams, is simply understood to be the way the game is played.

Of course, we tell ourselves—we EIA and CRM consultants—that we're only honest brokers. We look to see if there are any environmental impediments to our client's project, alert our client to them, and help our client figure out how to make them go away. The environment's protected and the project goes forward. Everybody wins. But it's not as simple as that.

Environmental impacts are often subtle things and open to interpretation—as are the rules, regulations, and standards by which we identify them and gauge their significance. The impacts we identify depend substantially on where we look, what we look at, how we look, what conceptual and analytic tools we use. They depend, in other words, on decisions we make. It's ridiculous to think that our decisions, our choices, aren't influenced by the interests of those whose financial support means the world to us.

Hypothetical example: Suppose we're looking at the impacts of a proposed small boat harbor along a river. The developer, our client, wants to build a jetty, and doing so requires a federal permit, or maybe our client is looking for a federal grant to help him build the jetty. Now, do we examine only the area where the jetty will be built to see whether there are endangered fish or fowl or mollusks there, or sunken historic steamboats? Or do we examine the impacts of the overall development, which wouldn't be economically viable if it didn't include the jetty? Do we think about where the boats that use the jetty are going to go, what erosion their wakes may cause, where their drivers may go ashore and pick flowers, camp, or dig for Indian artifacts? Do we examine how this development relates to the overall pattern of development up and down the river—whether it's part of a pattern of development that's cumulatively wiping out a habitat, a floodplain, a traditional pattern of human land use? If we consider these variables, *how* do we consider them? How far afield do we go in space, in time, in probability?

None of these questions have cut-and-dried, rigidly prescribed answers—though in certain circumstances, some are more prescribed than others. They all involve choices, based on our professional judgment. In making our choices, if we intend to keep our jobs, we have to factor in what our clients prefer. They almost certainly would prefer that we examine as narrow a range of impacts as possible, and find as few of them as we can.

All this has predictable consequences.

■ ■ ■ THE CONSEQUENCES

Launch a web search for "environmental impact statement" and a word like "ignore" or "distort," and you'll get many, many hits. Some are references to academic articles, quite a few are from other countries,[2] but many are information pages or expressions of alarm and outrage from citizens' groups, scholars, and legislators about twisted EIA work in the U.S. The cases vary, but the complaints are generally similar. About ten minutes with Google gave me accusations that federal agencies are ignoring or distorting the impacts of

◈ A liquefied natural gas terminal in Chesapeake Bay;[3]

◈ The fence that's supposed to halt illegal immigration across the border with Mexico;[4]

◈ Levees and locks on the Mississippi;[5]

◈ Disposal of nuclear waste in Nevada;[6]

◈ Mountaintop removal in Appalachia;[7]

◈ A big box store in New York City;[8]

◈ Navy missile testing in the Pacific.[9]

Some of these criticisms may not be justified, or at least there's doubtless another side to the stories they tell, but I'd give odds that few if any lack substantial grains of truth. And hidden under the abstract ascription of ill intent and action to "the agency," there are real people, mostly in consulting firms, who are conducting the studies and writing the reports that are accused of ignoring and distorting things.

It's not just big EIA studies that are accused of such abuses; I suspect they're actually more common on small projects, and in relatively narrow fields of study like CRM, where there aren't so many watchdog groups looking over agency shoulders. When people in the CRM world learned I was writing this book, they began to email me stories of waste, fraud, and corruption. No one wanted to be quoted, but they wanted me to know what they'd experienced. One reported an archaeological CRM firm whose people go to a client's proposed development site, take a few photos, and then fabricate site maps showing test pits they have supposedly excavated all over the site with negative results. "Developers love them," my correspondent said, "since they never find anything. They're paid very well." Another reported nearly being cashiered out of a job for telling a project opponent about some books (mine) that would help her understand NEPA and NHPA. Other reports were similar, from all over the country.

I haven't personally experienced quite such blatant abuses—or if I have, they've fooled me. What I see are subtler things—decisions about methods to employ, concepts to pay attention to, things to measure, that are influenced by what the consultant understands to be the client's desires. Abó Pass is a good example.

■ ■ ■ Abó Pass

Burlington Northern-Santa Fe Railway (BNSF), knowing that its Second Track project would have to cross a piece of federal land and fill some wetlands, understood that the Department of the Interior's Bureau of Land Management (BLM) and the U.S. Army Corps of Engineers would have to do some kind of EIA and CRM review. BLM would have to do so because issuing a right-of-way across federal land requires review under NEPA and section 106 of NHPA. As for the Corps, under section 404 of the Clean Water Act, anyone who wants to fill a wetland that's somehow connected to navigable waters in the United States must get the Corps' permission. In deciding whether to issue such a permit, the Corps has to consider the environmental impacts of the project that generates the need to fill the wetland. So it too has to review the project under NEPA and section 106

BNSF asked its engineering contractors to figure out what BLM and the Corps would need for their impact review, and to supply it. Informal discussions with local Corps and BLM staff guided the contractor in developing a scope of work, together with the contractor's and subcontractors' understanding of standard local practice. I'm most familiar with what the contractor did to find "cultural resources."

The contractors defined that term (implicitly; their documents didn't include an explicit definition) to include archaeological sites, historic structures, and (if the local tribes told them about any) sites of cultural or religious importance to Indian tribes.

Having thus defined away virtually anything cultural that wasn't an archaeological site or old building (and so eliminating the need to consider, for example, the overall landscape, the traditional ways of life of the ranchers, or tribal spiritual places unless a tribe pointed them out), the methods the contractors selected for finding "cultural resources" that might be affected were to conduct an archaeological field survey of the proposed project right-of-way plus a 50-foot "buffer" on either side of it, and to write letters to tribes, sometimes followed up with phone calls, to ask them about specific places they might be concerned about.

Having performed this work, they wrote a report, which BNSF filed with BLM and the Corps. The report identified the bridges and other structures associated with the original Santa Fe track—in active use though a century old—as cultural resources, together with several prehistoric and historic archaeological sites and pictographs—ancient paintings on overhangs along the canyon walls. The contractor proposed, and BNSF agreed, to route the tracks so as to avoid blowing up the pictograph sites and some of the archaeological sites. Other sites, along with the railroad facilities, would be excavated or otherwise documented before they were destroyed. Based on this "mitigation," they asserted that the project would have, in the words of the section 106 regulations, "no adverse effect on historic properties."[10]

There were several things wrong with the contractors' approach. Most obviously, you can't destroy an archaeological site, or anything else, and not have an adverse effect on it. If I burn your house to the ground, I've adversely affected it, no matter how well I may record it first. The regulations are reasonably clear about this self-evident fact. This may seem like a technicality, but had the "no adverse effect" determination stood, under the section 106 regulations that would have been the end of it. The project could have proceeded with no further government oversight as far as section 106 requirements were concerned—provided BNSF performed the rather minor design and documentation work its contractors proposed (assuming the Corps actually required it to do so).

The determination did not stand, so there's no way of knowing exactly what would have happened if it had, but the point is that the contractors were proposing a quick, easy, relatively inexpensive way for their client to get through the review process and move forward. There's nothing necessarily wrong with that, but in this case what may have been a responsible concern for the client's bottom line led the consultants to propose work that was (a) flatly inconsistent with the regulations[11] and (b) didn't reveal all the project's impacts on "cultural resources."

The project would cut a huge swath through the landscape of Abó Pass—quite a distinctive landform with a long history of human use. The pass is currently used for cattle ranching, a rather important traditional activity in New Mexico, and some of the ranchers are Hispanic families that have been on the land for three and four generations. Were these not "cultural resources" that would be affected? What about culturally important plants and animals? What about the relationships among all these things in the landscape? What about the landscape of the pass itself, its landforms, its vistas?

Specialists can argue about this sort of thing, and of course we have, but what's striking is that the contractors apparently didn't even *consider* looking beyond their narrow corridor, at anything larger than or different from an archaeological site or old structure. Nor did they consider anything but direct impacts—what would be blown up, knocked down, bulldozed. Although the regulations for both NEPA and section 106 of NHPA require addressing all kinds of impacts—direct, indirect, and cumulative effects— everything other than direct physical effects was glossed over. Visual effects, audible effects, the effects of blasting vibrations on pictographs, the cumulative effects of a century of railroad use on the canyon—all were ignored.

The argument over what was in fact culturally significant in Abó Pass, and what ought to be done to determine how it would be affected, was joined only because the Rosas objected to what the project would do to their land, and engaged their own consultant—me—to analyze what BNSF's contractors had done and written. BNSF's contractors, to judge from their reports, would have analyzed only direct impacts in a narrow corridor, only on specific archaeological sites and historic structures— unless a tribe told them about something else, and it is doubtful that such information would be volunteered had the Rosas not independently contacted tribes and alerted them to the impacts of the project.

But the Rosas did object, did notify the tribes, did lobby the Corps and BLM to look more broadly and carefully at the project's impacts, did raise objections with the State Historic Preservation Officer (SHPO) and Advisory Council on Historic Preservation (ACHP), did enlist the aid of the National Trust for Historic Preservation (NTHP). This resulted in an archaeological examination of a somewhat broader corridor, some face-to-face consultation with tribes, some interviews with local ranchers and other residents, and a good deal of argument among specialists, in which BNSF's contractors consistently represented their clients' interests.

One can hardly fault the contractors for this. After all, they were working for BNSF. But that, of course, is the point. How can one possibly expect contractors not to try to get the best deal they can for their client? The client's project, after all, means the world to them.

Buckland

The situation in northern Virginia is much the same as in New Mexico, though rather more institutionalized. It's not uncommon for development interests to have subsidiaries that do engineering, architecture, and planning. These companies routinely conduct EIA and CRM work, or have more or less standing contracts with EIA and CRM specialists. The subsidiaries provide services to others, but they're always on hand to perform whatever studies their parent companies require. For some reason, this does not seem to raise eyebrows among the oversight and regulatory agencies.

It's these firms that have routinely done the studies required by the Corps of Engineers, Federal Highway Administration, and other agencies responsible for NEPA and section 106 compliance around Buckland. And—what do you know?—they've consistently found the battlefield to be smaller than other experts have found it to be, conveniently excluding their clients' proposed development areas. When challenged, and confronted with solid evidence that their judgments have been wrong, they've tended to lose the paperwork or forget to respond.

As in the case of Abó Pass, the northern Virginia consulting firms have also downplayed or simply ignored impacts that aren't blatantly obvious and direct. One thing that's particularly striking at Buckland is the strange ways that cumulative effects are considered—or not.

Cumulative effects, in the words of the NEPA regulations, are the effects of a given project on a given area or type of resource when combined with all other past, present, and reasonably foreseeable future effects.[12] That may sound pretty esoteric, but it's a very important concept, especially in a place like northern Virginia. While each housing tract or gas station or fast-food joint may not have much impact on the environment *all by itself, cumulatively* the effect of them all may be devastating. Building the Big Bag Grocery Store just up the road from the Buckland Mills Battlefield may not by itself greatly damage the area's historic character, but transformation of the area neither starts nor stops with the Big Bag. There's the new sewer that went in a couple of years ago, and the new housing tract that was made possible by the sewer, whose residents will shop at the Big Bag. There's the shopping mall that someone plans to put in across the road, and the light industrial park a quarter mile away. All these projects have synergistic relationships with one another, and the result—cumulatively—is that the area is fundamentally changed. Maybe it's a change for the better, at least in some people's eyes; it's certainly a change for the worse in the eyes of the Buckland Preservation Society. Good or bad, it's an effect, and analyzing effects is what EIA and CRM are supposed to do. Cumulative effects analysis—if it's done properly—tries to get a handle on how a given project fits into the overall pattern of incremental, accumulating change. Will it make the overall effect worse? Will it somehow reduce or redirect it? Are there mitigation measures that can be employed? There may or may not be good and useful answers to these questions, but if they're not asked, if the analysis isn't done, answers can't possibly be found.

Ordinarily, the consultants for developers and agencies in northern Virginia pretty much ignore cumulative effects, or just throw the words into their reports without saying anything meaningful or even sensible. It's common to turn the whole idea of cumulative effects analysis on its head, in essence saying "there's been lots of development around here, so more development won't have any significant effects." We'll look at a particularly egregious example of twisted cumulative effects "analysis" in the next chapter. For now, suffice it to say that minimizing recognition of such effects is standard operating procedure for EIA and CRM consultants in northern Virginia, and people who value places like Buckland suffer as a result.

The Topock Maze

At the Topock Maze, the EIA and CRM contractors were hired by Pacific Gas and Electric Company, the firm responsible for the toxic chromium spill and for its cleanup. To the considerable dismay of the Fort Mojave Indian Tribe, they treated the Maze as an archaeological site, ignoring the cultural value ascribed by the tribe to the landscape that encompassed it. The Tribe's efforts to get the contractors or their client to appreciate the overall landscape were met with blank looks and assurances that individual archaeological sites would not be drilled into.

To understand how this sort of thing feels to the Fort Mojave people, imagine you're a devout Christian, and somebody proposes to drill holes in the floor of your church to get at something toxic that's thought to lie underneath. You may not want the toxics to stay there, so you may agree that some kind of drilling ought to be done, but you'd probably like it to be done in a way that somehow respects your beliefs about the sanctity of the church.

"No problem," says the driller. "We'll have our cultural resource experts deal with it." Whereupon they bring in experts in mosaic floor design and the construction of church pews, who develop an elaborate plan for drilling in ways that won't disturb the specific physical features *they* think are important. Never mind that *you* think, for instance, that the way the light shines through the southeast stained-glass window onto the floor of the nave is especially important; the nave is clear for drilling as far as the experts are concerned. And never mind that you'd rather they didn't drill on the sabbath.

You'd be outraged at this, of course, and so is the Fort Mojave Indian Tribe—at PG&E, the Bureau of Land Management (BLM), and their CRM contractors. But the contractors are just trying to minimize costs and trouble for their client, and using their particular kinds of expertise to do so. The Fort Mojave Indian Tribe has to struggle mightily to get anyone to pay attention to its concerns, and it's gotten no help from PG&E's consultants.

It's really pretty simple. When a specialist is hired by a project proponent, no matter how skilled, professional, and even honorable that specialist may be, he or she can't help but be influenced by the client's interest in moving his or her project forward quickly and at least cost. In some ways, it's only right that this should be the case. But it can't possibly produce a balanced, unbiased interpretation of environmental impacts, and it's the way most EIA and CRM work is done in the United States.

There are exceptions. Some agencies—BLM does this in some states—routinely insist that environmental and cultural resource studies be done by contractors who report directly to BLM, rather than to the project proponent. The proponent pays, but the agency calls the shots. Sometimes, however—as we'll see in Chapter Seven—the ostensibly independent "third party" contractor for the agency turns out to be the very firm that is also under contract with the proponent.

In most cases, though, work under the heritage laws is done by contractors for project proponents, and even the most honorable contractor—perhaps *especially* the most honorable contractor—has to be strongly influenced by his client's expressed interests and desires.

▪ ▪ ▪ INTEGRITY AND THE BOTTOM LINE

At the beginning of this chapter I quoted an important line from the NEPA regulations of the Council on Environmental Quality (CEQ). They're worth repeating:

> Agencies shall insure the professional integrity, including scientific integrity, of the discussions and analyses in environmental impact statements.[13]

One could split hairs here and point out that I haven't been talking in this chapter about doing environmental impact *statements,* but environmental *assessments* and CRM studies. That *would* be splitting hairs, however, and giving far too much attention to what amounts to some inartful regulation-writing on CEQ's part. When the regulations were written, back in the 1970s, CEQ expected that environmental impact statements (EISs) would be the usual vehicle for NEPA analysis; as a result, the regulations go into great detail about how EISs should be done, and pay little attention to what has turned out to be far more commonly performed types of NEPA practice—doing environmental assessments (EAs) and screening categorically excluded projects for "extraordinary circumstances." But if integrity—that is, honesty and balance in the assessment of impacts—is important in preparing an EIS, it hardly makes sense to think it is not equally important in deciding whether an

EIS is necessary—and in analyzing impacts on particular aspects of the environment, like "cultural resources."

I think it's safe to say that the authors of the NEPA regulations, and of NEPA—and, for that matter, the authors of NHPA and the Endangered Species Act and all the rest—expected that EIA practitioners would do their work with integrity. Unfortunately, such integrity is less and less evident in our practice. We EIA and CRM specialists seem to have concluded that it's our clients' projects that "mean the world to us"—not the world's environment itself.

■ ■ ■ "PEOPLE ARE REALLY GOOD AT HEART"

So wrote Anne Frank shortly before the Gestapo came for her. But it would be nice to think she was right at some level. I don't think my fellow EIA and CRM consultants—or I, for that matter—are evil people. I simply think we are trapped in an inherently corrupt system and have gotten so used to it that most of us don't even recognize we have a problem. Most of us, I'm convinced, think we're doing right.

I recently gave a short talk to a group of CRM consultants in which I outlined some of this book's main premises. During the comment period, one fellow—with much head-nodding by others in the room—insisted that consultants are not *supposed* to be objective analysts of impacts. "That's the federal agency's job," he said. "We do the best we can for our client; the people who oppose the project make their case, and the agency weighs and balances things and makes its decision."

I'll get to the agencies in the next chapter, but I think the commenter—while certainly speaking honestly and in good faith—was misled. NEPA and section 106 do indeed expect that federal agencies will make balanced decisions after weighing and balancing all the relevant factors—environmental, economic, social, political. But agencies are not staffed, funded, or organized to collect the data needed to reach such decisions, so they contract for the EIA and CRM work, or task non-federal project proponents to do so. In theory, the consultants thus contracted are doing the *agency decision maker's* work, not the project proponent's. And it's the project proponents who have the money to hire the consultants;

project opponents, on the whole, do not. Plus, as we'll see, the opponents often don't even know what's going on and are seldom well versed in CRM and EIA. If NEPA and section 106 are games played between project proponents and opponents with federal agencies as referees, they're played on a steeply sloped field, between very unevenly matched teams.

But still, I do not accuse my commenter, or his colleagues, or even myself, of being out to screw over the environment for a buck. We're just doing what we're used to doing, in a system that's evolved into something much different from what the authors of NEPA and NHPA had in mind.

Three   Reviewers as Advocates

All agencies of the Federal Government shall . . . utilize a systematic, interdisciplinary approach which will insure the integrated use of the natural and social sciences and the environmental design arts in planning and decision-making which may have an impact on man's environment.

National Environmental Policy Act, sec. 102

"Systematic, interdisciplinary approach" . . . "integrated use of the . . . sciences and arts." This sort of language suggests, and indeed both NEPA and NHPA assume, that federal agencies consider the impacts of proposed projects in a thorough, balanced, thoughtful, unbiased manner. We've seen that the consultants collecting the data and doing the analyses don't necessarily give agencies much to work with, but what about the agencies themselves? How balanced and objective is the exercise of their analytic responsibilities? Let's look at some examples.

THE DISAPPEARING TRAIN WRECK

Back in November 1983, a freight train left the track in Abó Canyon. Fifty-six of the train's seventy-four cars derailed and tumbled into the arroyo.[1] The train was loaded mostly with automobiles, though there was apparently at least one tank car loaded with petroleum naphtha; witnesses said that flames shot hundreds of feet into the air and that the canyon looked like a "fiery hell."[2] The canyon walls still show signs of scorching.

The accident briefly received nationwide attention on the "NBC Nightly News," and there was coverage in the local papers, but BNSF's predecessor, the Atcheson Topeka and Santa Fe, closed the canyon to visitors and cleaned up the mess. No one in government seems to have looked into how the cleanup was done. Ranchers living in the area at the time say the railroad pulled out what it could and then bulldozed huge trenches and buried the rest. Today there are fragments of rail cars and automobiles sticking out of the arroyo banks.

Needless to say, the derailment site—which would be disturbed by construction of the new track along one of the alignments under consideration—was a matter of concern to the Rosas. They asked the Corps to make sure it was looked into, so that if there were toxic or hazardous materials buried at the site, they wouldn't get released in the course of construction. The response from the Corps:

> [W]ork being conducted (bulldozing to remove salt cedar) has uncovered some automobile parts along Abó Arroyo. Some of these car parts may be related to the previous train derailment in Abó Canyon, while some of the parts may be due to the common practice in the past of disposing of old automobiles in arroyos in New Mexico. The Corps does not believe that the uncovering of these parts requires additional soil or water testing at the site.[3]

There may have been good reasons not to worry about pollution from the derailment site (but see Chapter Five), but the possibility that the wreckage in the arroyo resulted from someone's illicit auto dumping was not one of them. The site is miles from any even semi-public road, is the precise scene of the 1983 derailment, and to judge from my own observations, exhibits a more impressive array of rail car parts than it does fragments of Fords. The Corps, in short, was reaching pretty far to cover its eyes. Why? We can't know, but it doesn't take much imagination to guess. If the Corps had allowed itself to take the derailment site seriously as a possible source of pollution, they would have had to consider whether BNSF's project might release toxic material into the soil and water. And they would have had to ask some probing questions of BNSF, which says it has no records of the derailment and cleanup. The Corps saw it as its job to expedite issuing BNSF a permit, and nothing like a little possible toxic waste site could be allowed to get in the way.

Agency advocacy of projects whose impacts they are supposed to analyze objectively is usually more subtly expressed than this, and more subtly experienced by the agency and its employees. But it's there, and it strongly influences the way the agency does its job—as the Buckland Preservation Society (BPS) has learned.

Buckland and the Corps

In trying to preserve the village of Buckland and the Buckland Mills Battlefield, the BPS involves itself in NHPA and NEPA review mostly through two federal agencies. One is the Federal Highway Administration, whose assistance to the Virginia Department of Transportation makes it possible for roads and highways to be built and improved in the area, allowing more traffic to flow through, which allows more houses and malls to be constructed. The other agency is—as at Abó Canyon—the Corps of Engineers. Northern Virginia has a lot of wetlands, so many, if not most, development projects need permits under section 404 of the Clean Water Act. When the Corps considers issuing a permit, it has to look at the impacts of doing so, under NEPA and section 106 of NHPA.

▪ ▪ ▪ THE TROUBLE WITH SECTION 404

Pun intended, the Corps feels it is on rather shaky ground in carrying out such reviews—and it has good reasons for that feeling. The Corps' permitting authority comes ultimately, if counterintuitively, from the U.S. Constitution's "commerce clause." The commerce clause reserves to the federal government the authority to manage commerce between the states, with foreign nations, and with Indian tribes. Commerce is to some extent dependent on rivers, canals, and other water bodies, and hence on water. This has long been understood to give the federal government the right to regulate actions affecting to navigable waters in rivers and harbors. There is no clause in the Constitution giving Congress the right to protect the environment, so when it concluded that something had to be done about the quality of the nation's water, Congress leaned on the commerce clause. Navigable waters would go dry and hence become non-navigable if they weren't regularly recharged by waterbodies upstream— such as wetlands. Hence, in order to responsibly regulate navigable waters in the interests of orderly commerce, Congress could and did, under section 404, assert the federal government's authority to regulate filling wetlands. Section 404 is frequently challenged in court, and the Corps' jurisdiction under it is pretty regularly constrained. This makes the Corps understandably gun-shy. It really doesn't want well-heeled developers with fancy law firms challenging its authority, so it usually tries very hard to stay out of trouble with project proponents.

But for a group like the BPS, section 404 review by the Corps is often—usually—the only way to get a private development's impacts on the environment reviewed at all. In northern Virginia, as throughout the South, any sort of limit on private property rights is viewed with great suspicion, so state and local regulatory authority is—to put it politely— very limited. Philosophically, one can just shrug and say that's the way it is, and live elsewhere—that's what I do. But if for some reason you want to live in Virginia, and want to protect your environment, you have to look to laws like NEPA and section 106 for help. The Corps' section 404 review is the federal "handle" that makes it possible to apply these laws.

The BPS is involved in section 404 reviews constantly—usually several at a time. It typically goes like this. Developer A, who wants to put in a housing project on or close to the Buckland Mills Battlefield and who needs to fill a wetland to do it, applies to the Corps for a permit. The Corps has a routine process for issuing permits. Once it receives a complete application, it puts out a public notice and tells the applicant to conduct studies to characterize the project's environmental impacts. Based on public comments, it may ask the developer to do further studies. Based on the information thus collected, and what the developer proposes to do to limit and/or compensate for the wetlands they are going to eliminate, the Corps decides whether to issue the permit, and what conditions to impose if—as is almost always the case—it is issued.

Being edgy about the limits of its jurisdiction, the Corps tends not to ask applicants to do very much when it comes to impact review, and tries to make the whole business as routine as possible. And its inclination is to issue a requested permit unless virtually forced to do otherwise.

So here's what happened in one fairly recent case. I'll generalize about it and refrain from naming names; there's no one more litigious than a northern Virginia land developer.

∎ ∎ ∎ GEORGE THE DEVELOPER AND THE PROBLEM OF CUMULATIVE EFFECT

The developer—let's call him George—proposed to put in a development on a piece of vacant land west of Buckland. Part of the parcel was rather marshy—a wetland by the Corps' definition. George couldn't build his project without filling the wetland, so he needed a permit from the Corps. He applied for one, and the Corps told him to conduct studies as a basis for review under NEPA and section 106 of NHPA. The Corps issued a public notice letting people know that the application had been filed and giving them a standard period of time—thirty days, with some possibility for extensions—in which to comment.

BPS expressed its concern that the development would have adverse effects on Buckland and the Buckland Mills Battlefield—primarily because it would continue and exacerbate the cumulative pattern of sprawl development that threatens to overwhelm the area and fundamentally alter its character.

We discussed cumulative effects a little in the last chapter, but let's consider them in a bit more detail. The NEPA regulations define "cumulative impact" as

> the impact on the environment which results from the incremental impact of the action when added to other past, present, and reasonably foreseeable future actions regardless of what agency (Federal or non-Federal) or person undertakes such other actions. Cumulative impacts can result from individually minor but collectively significant actions taking place over a period of time.
>
> *40 CFR 1508.7*

The regulations, incidentally, use "impact" and "effect" interchangeably. The NHPA section 106 regulations use the same term without defining it, but the Advisory Council on Historic Preservation (ACHP)—the section 106 rulemaking body, remember—has said that whenever its regulations use a NEPA term and don't define it differently, the definitions in the NEPA regulations apply.

Cumulative effects are tricky to deal with, but they're tremendously important, and a place like northern Virginia illustrates why. A given development—a new road, a sewer extension, a housing tract or shopping mall or grocery store or fast-food shop—may by itself be pretty benign in terms of environmental impacts; so if you consider them only one by one, on their own independent merits and impacts, you're likely to let them go in. Then one day you wake up and—wow, the whole county's been paved over! That's cumulative effect. Someone once said it was like being nibbled to death by ducks.

But, of course, an agency like the Corps handles permit applications on a case-by-case basis; there's nothing else it can do. So how can it deal with cumulative effects? The regulations don't say, but they *do* say that the Corps, like any other agency, has to consider them, weigh and balance them, in making its permit decisions.

Bombing Boise

The Corps doesn't like to think about cumulative effects. Maybe no agency does, but the Corps gets particularly miffed at having to do so. "It's not our business," they say in essence; "it's for local planning and zoning to deal with." Or "it's not our business because we don't regulate most of the developments that have effects; they're outside our jurisdiction."

Both arguments are about half right. Certainly it is the job of local planning and zoning authorities to worry about the cumulative effects of development and other changing land uses, but that doesn't mean that the federal government shouldn't think about how *its* decisions, *its* actions, may contribute to such effects. Certainly, too, much of the development that goes on in an area like northern Virginia is outside the Corps' jurisdiction. But when it enacted NEPA and NHPA, Congress didn't say "agencies shall consider the effects of their actions provided they have jurisdiction over such effects." Congress said to consider effects, period.

Why would Congress direct agencies to consider effects that they lack the jurisdiction to do anything about? Two reasons. First, if it can do nothing else, an agency can just say no to a proposed project that it finds will contribute to adverse cumulative (or other) effects. In the case of the Corps, it can deny the permit. Second, if the agency starts thinking about the problem, and talking with others about it, it may find that there are actions that *others* can and will take to address it, and it may encourage them to do so.

Imagine, for example, that what developer George proposed to do on his wetland was build a launch site for a nuclear-tipped missile that he would fling across the country and drop on Boise, Idaho. The Corps' section 404 authorities don't have anything to do with controlling nuclear weapons, and the Corps in Virginia has no jurisdiction over things that happen in Boise, but does that mean the Corps shouldn't consider what would happen if George were allowed to put in his pad and push his button? Of course it doesn't. In the first place, the Corps can deny George the permit, which may at least slow him down. Second, if the Corps starts talking with George and others about the matter—*consulting,* as section 106 requires—someone may talk George out of pursuing his adventure, or someone may get involved in the consultation who *does* have jurisdiction and *can* do something. The Air Force, perhaps, or the police, or the Idaho Militia.

In just the same way, the Corps can deny George's permit to put in his development, if cumulative effects analysis indicates that issuing it will open the floodgates to sprawl that overwhelms the character of the Buckland Mills Battlefield. And if the Corps were to open consultation on the project and bring local government to the table, it—or other consulting parties, like BPS or the State Historic Preservation officer—might be able to prevail on the county to change its planning and zoning.

There's another possibility, too. The Corps could step back and say, "Y'know, we're seeing a lot of projects like George's in this area, and the overall effects are pretty evident. Rather than doing case-by-case review, which obscures these effects, we're going to lump applications together and review them all on a quarterly basis, together, in consultation with local government, the state, and the citizens. We're going to focus on the synergistic relationships among them and how they all relate to what people want the area to look like in the long-term." I'm sure there are administrative impediments to doing something like this, and maybe it's a bad idea, but my point is simply that the Corps isn't necessarily bound to do the same old thing time after time. It *could* be creative and perhaps better and more efficiently meet the responsibilities that Congress really did give it—and the federal government as a whole—in section 101 of NEPA.

No Foreseeable Development in Northern Virginia

So like it or not, the Corps has to consider cumulative effects in its NEPA and section 106 reviews. But it doesn't like it and looks for ways to do as little of it as possible. So how could it minimize attention to cumulative effects in the case of George's development?

Past effects on the area are pretty hard to miss. For much of the twentieth century there was small-scale development throughout the area—a house here, a gas station there—but most of the land was in stable agricultural use. After World War II, though, development took off throughout northern Virginia, and the leading edge of suburbia has crept steadily closer.

Current impacts are also easy to see, if one looks. Development was and is spreading down the highway; traffic was and is increasing; noise and congestion and all the other concomitants of suburbanization are growing, property values and assessments are rising, tempting or forcing more and more landowners to sell, subdivide, or develop their lands. A great environment for George, but getting steadily less and less conducive to preserving the traditional character of Buckland and the battlefield.

These things were obvious as the Corps began review of George's project. And at least insofar as people like the BPS members forced them to, the Corps had to consider them. Sort of. To the extent the Corps and George's consultants can get away with thinking, talking, and writing about them in only vague, abstract terms, they can emasculate concepts like cumulative effects, let the air out of them, keep the destruction they

represent from really being grasped. It helps to play scientist and emphasize quantitative variables, particularly if you can't actually find anything
to quantify. "Sprawl? Well, yeah, there's sprawl, but how much does new
housing contribute to it? Gee, we really don't know, and since we can't
come up with a formula, we really can't include it in our impact assessment."

But the past is gone and the present is here; *future* effects were where
the rubber really met the road with George's proposal. How could these
be identified?

One obvious way was to look at local planning and zoning. What did
the county government's planning office predict? Unsurprisingly, the
county's plans for the future—maybe twenty or thirty years out—showed
the area pretty much built up, sprawled over, with an equivocal sort of
bow toward maybe trying to keep the battlefield or some part of it as
open space. There were pretty specific plans for the lands around and
including George's proposed development site, showing a network of pro-
jected streets along which houses and businesses would spring up.

Cumulative effects, you'll recall, according to the Council on
Environmental Quality, include past, present, and *reasonably foreseeable*
future effects. Now, you might think that development mapped in the
county's planning documents is pretty foreseeable, but the Corps had a
talk with the county planning staff, who said (according to the Corps)
that they didn't really expect those roads to be built, or that development
to occur, any time soon. They're in our plans, sure, but don't take them
seriously.

That's that, the Corps told BPS in an on-site meeting; the development isn't reasonably foreseeable, so we don't have to consider it.

Ironically, in the same meeting the Corps argued that since county
planning indicated the battlefield as open space, it was going to be preserved, so the BPS had no basis for complaint. The Corps could and
would rely on county planning as evidence to back up its decision to issue
the permit, while denying its relevance as a rationale for (maybe, possibly,
conceivably) even *considering* denying it.

So the Corps issued the permit, and George's development has gone
ahead, with all its contributions to the transformation of the Buckland

area into another bit of suburbia. Maybe that was inevitable, maybe it's even the right thing to happen in some great scheme of things, but it certainly doesn't resemble an honest, balanced consideration of effects.

Agency bias in favor of development interests is hardly unique to the Corps, Virginia, or urban development. In my experience, it's almost universal among federal agencies, regardless of whether they're considering their own projects or regulating someone else's. And like consultant bias, it's accepted by almost everyone as just The Way Things Are.

■ ■ ■ "WE'LL DO OUR EA AND ISSUE OUR FONSI"

Agencies can be pretty blatant about their bias, though they'll always give lip service to objectivity and serving the public interest. In the course of the Abó Canyon case, the Rosas' attorney regularly filed requests for paperwork from the Corps of Engineers under the Freedom of Information Act (FOIA), which—more or less and subject to quite a few exceptions—requires federal agencies to provide the public with copies of the documents they collect and generate. One document the FOIA requests produced was an internal Corps memorandum neatly demonstrating how open-minded the Corps and Bureau of Land Management (BLM) were in examining BNSF Railroad's proposed project.

You'll recall that when an agency isn't sure whether a project will have a significant effect on the quality of the human environment,[4] and hence will require preparation of an environmental impact statement (EIS), it does an environmental assessment (EA). An EA is supposed to be a brief but thorough (and implicitly, objective) analysis of a project's likely effects. It's supposed to be the basis for a decision by the agency as to whether significant effects are likely. If they are, the agency is required to do an EIS. If they're not, the agency issues a "finding of no significant impact"—a FONSI.

According to the Corps memo, representatives of the Corps, BLM, and BNSF met on March 29, 2006, to discuss how things were progressing on compliance with NEPA, the Endangered Species Act (ESA), and section 106 of NHPA. Regarding NEPA, the memo says:

The BLM stated that they are waiting on the receipt of the draft EA being prepared by [BNSF's environmental contractor]. They said that this document needs to discuss the completion of the Section 106 and Section 7 [sic: Endangered Species Act] processes. The BLM said that their EA will be sent out for a 30-day public review, prior to the signing of a finding of no significant impact (FONSI).[5]

So before BLM had even received a draft of the EA from the contractor—BNSF's contractor, that is—who was preparing it, the Corps, BLM, and BNSF took it for granted that BLM was going to issue a FONSI—that is, find that the project would have no significant impact on the human environment.

In point of fact—and as documented to some extent in the draft EA published two years later (with many interesting omissions; see Chapter Seven)—the project's dramatic cuts and fills would markedly change the character of the canyon; it would affect bighorn sheep habitat, destroy early Pueblo archaeological sites, threaten ancient rock art, alter the traditional use of the area by ranchers, and possibly release into the environment whatever was in the buried rail cars from the 1983 derailment. But what's important here is that although neither the Corps nor BLM had carried out the assessment that was both legally and logically necessary to determine whether all these effects amounted to something significant, they already knew they were going to find them not so. In short, the fix was in.

This is by no means uncommon. I've seen requests for proposals (RFPs) in which the agency seeking a contractor specified that the contractor would prepare an EA and FONSI, and I've very, very rarely seen a case in which an EA actually led to the decision to do an EIS. It does happen, but usually only with a lot of pressure from outside the agency.

Obfuscating Alternatives

Both the NEPA and section 106 regulations require the consideration of alternatives. The importance of alternatives is especially stressed under NEPA, where—at least when you're doing an EIS—you're first supposed to establish the "purpose and need" for the action—what it's for, why it's needed—and then explore a range of ways to achieve that purpose, meet that need. Unfortunately, the NEPA regulations are a lot more vague about whether alternatives have to be considered when doing an EA, and the section 106 regulations just use the word from time to time.

Project proponents tend to feel pretty confident that the project they've decided on is the best or only way to achieve their purpose and meet their needs. They tend to see it as a waste of time and money to consider alternative ways of getting there. Where the proponent is a private party—Developer George in Virginia, BNSF Railway in New Mexico, PG&E on the Colorado River—they've often invested a lot of money in their selected alternative before review under NEPA and section 106 ever begins. In theory, what a responsible federal agency ought to do is insist that a reasonable range of alternatives be examined, so it can be sure that the one selected is really in the public interest. There's some case law, and it's ostensible policy in some agencies, indicating that a more or less equal level of analysis ought to be given to all alternatives that aren't thoroughly ridiculous; but the focus of this kind of policy is on EIS preparation, and an agency that's committed to an EA and FONSI is by definition not going to do an EIS.

Where an agency is predisposed to approve a project, it's likely to minimize consideration of alternatives, focusing on small, tweaking variations of the "preferred" alternative" and burying more substantial alternatives as deeply as possible. Again, Abó Pass provides a classic example.

■ ■ ■ A TUNNEL IS A TUNNEL IS A TUNNEL

BNSF's preferred alternative for its Second Track project—its only alternative, truthfully, though there were minor variants on the theme—was a new set of cuts and fills, embankments and bridges, that would weave around the existing track, sometimes on one side, sometimes on the other. It would involve blasting back the canyon walls along the right-of-way, turning the landscape from something more or less natural—even with the existing track—into something closely resembling an interstate highway. The Rosas felt that there ought to be some less damaging way to accomplish BNSF's purpose, meet BNSF's need. They didn't question that purpose or need; freight has to be hauled, and BNSF's shareholders have a right to seek a profit. But did the whole canyon have to be transformed to achieve these purposes?

Why, for example, couldn't the second track be laid directly adjacent to the first track, just widening the right of way without so much cutting and filling? Not feasible, BNSF said, because we'd have to stop train traffic too often during construction; it wouldn't be cost effective. Which of course may be true, but what's notable is that the Corps accepted the railroad's premise without batting an eye. The Rosas rolled theirs, however, and kept pressing the Corps to look at alternatives. Finally, one of the Corps' environmental staff members said, in essence, look, if you want the railroad to consider an alternative, you're going to have to give them one to consider; you'll have to develop a plan for one and show it to us.

If you think about it for a moment, this was a pretty outrageous suggestion. It was the railroad that wanted to rip up the landscape to enhance the profitability of its operations. It was the Corps that was responsible for deciding whether the railroad's proposal was sufficiently in the public interest to justify filling a protected wetland. It was BLM that was responsible for a similar decision about the justification for taking a chunk of public land. All the Rosas were doing was trying to keep their ranch and its environment from being chopped up. To achieve this purpose, they had already invested a lot of time, trouble, and the money to hire lawyers and consultants like me. Why in the world should *they* be responsible for coming up with alternatives for the railroad to consider?

But they did it. They looked around for an engineer they could hire to explore lower-impact ways to get a railroad track from one end of the canyon to the other. Finding such an engineer was not easy—both because there aren't many engineers with the requisite special expertise, and because, as the Rosas discovered, not many engineers wanted to get crosswise with the railroad.

Eventually, the Rosas found Dr. Kamran Nemati, a civil engineer on the faculty of the Department of Construction and Civil Engineering at the University of Washington. Dr. Nemati was on sabbatical in Japan, but he agreed to come visit the canyon, look the situation over, review the railroad's data, and see what he could come up with. He did, and what he concluded surprised both the Rosas and me. He suggested a tunnel.

A short tunnel was included in one of BNSF's alternatives, a tweaking of the "preferred" right-of-way that would cut through a bend in the canyon, but BNSF regarded it as not feasible. From the Rosas' perspective, it didn't make much difference; the bulk of the line would still be at-grade, doing all the damage that at-grade construction involved. What Dr. Nemati proposed was something quite different. Tunneling technology, he said, has progressed so far that it is entirely feasible to bore under an entire area like Abó Pass using automated boring equipment that chews through the rock and lines the tunnel with cement as it goes. Think about the Channel Tunnel between England and France, the Loetschberg Tunnel under the Alps, or, for that matter, any number of deep rapid-rail tunnels under cities like Washington, DC. Certainly it would cost more than building at-grade, but in the long run it might very well save BNSF money. A tunnel could be straighter than a surface route, its grade could be flatter, so trains could move faster through it; therefore you could move more trains and thus more freight, more quickly than the at-grade alternative would allow. You wouldn't have rockslides blocking the tracks, or bighorn sheep falling on them off the cliffs, or cattle wandering onto them. And in terms of security—a serious issue for an industry that emphasizes its contribution to the nation's economy—it is a whole lot easier to protect two tunnel entrances from terrorists than it is to protect a long, winding route through a tortuous canyon.

So Dr. Nemati prepared a report that outlined conceptual plans for two alternatives, as examples of what might be done. There was a relatively long South Alternative that tunneled under the whole pass, and a shorter North Alternative that went under only the ruggedest, most difficult-to-build-through segment, which also was the most scenic and contained most of the bighorn sheep habitat and culturally significant landscape.

He also mentioned something in passing to the Rosas—it never got into his report—that I found intriguing. Like much of the railroad infrastructure in the country, he said, it was probable that BNSF's existing track through the canyon was approaching the end of its useful life. It's a hundred years old, after all. The concrete bridge piers are smeared with epoxy to hold them together. If BNSF were really thinking long-term, he implied, they might want to consider putting both tracks in tunnels, getting out of the canyon altogether. This alternative, of course, would free the canyon up for other uses—ranching, recreation, a tourist trail or train along the old grade, and so on. It certainly seemed worth thinking about.

The Rosas went further to check out the viability of the Nemati tunnel alternatives. They contracted with a tunneling expert, Gordon Clark, to review Nemati's report and BNSF's, and come to his own conclusions. Clark said that Nemati's approach made sense to him, though once detailed studies had been done, of course, it might turn out to be infeasible, given the specific nature of the rock to be tunneled through and a range of other factors. The alternative certainly deserved consideration, he said—that "hard look" that the courts have said agencies are to give project impacts and alternatives under NEPA.

So the Rosas submitted the Nemati report and Clark's comments to the Corps and asked them—as the Corps of *Engineers,* after all—to give the alternative a careful engineering analysis.

The Corps said its engineers didn't do that. Only the environmental staff gets involved with environmental matters, and they don't have any engineering expertise. But that was OK, they would just ask BNSF for *its* analysis.

Which they did, and to no one's surprise, BNSF's engineer, Robert Boileau, said the tunnels were totally impractical, much too expensive, wouldn't work, and would do as much damage as at-grade construction. They'd be hard to maintain, they'd be dangerous, they'd flood, they'd asphyxiate the train crews. BNSF had already considered tunneling in great detail when they were designing their own tunnel alternative and concluded that it just wouldn't work.

Nemati and Clark said they were talking about really different kinds of tunnels; what applied to BNSF's proposed old-style excavation of a nearly at-grade tunnel through a bend in the canyon didn't compare with boring under the whole pass with modern technology. BNSF said they'd really analyzed tunnels enough and wanted to get on with building their railroad. The Corps had nothing substantive to say.

The Rosas managed to arrange a meeting and flew Gordon Clark out to New Mexico. BNSF repeated its claims, Clark offered rebuttals, and the Corps, I'm told, sat and listened.

And concluded, they said, that there really wasn't much difference between the Nemati tunnels and the tunnel BNSF had already considered. Since they'd already decided that the BNSF tunnel wasn't worth detailed consideration, the Nemati alternatives weren't either. Case closed.

Now, it may be that the Nemati tunnels really weren't feasible; maybe they weren't good alternatives. But does the analysis of one engineer employed by the project proponent constitute the sort of "hard look" that agencies are supposed to give projects and alternatives? Was the Corps— of *Engineers*—really exercising its independent judgment in the public interest when it wouldn't assign one of its own engineers to analyze the alternatives? Was it really doing its job under NEPA and section 106? Or was it just trying to generate the impression of compliance with the heritage laws while doing as little as possible to get in BNSF's way? Was it an objective reviewer of the project's impacts, or an advocate for the project?

■ ■ ■ MORE ROADS TO ADVOCACY

There are other ways that federal agencies can facilitate projects without seriously considering their effects—whether the projects are their own or those of parties they oversee.

Divvy It Up and Put It Off

If you can divide a big project or program into little pieces and analyze the effects of each one separately, the effects will be a lot less impressive than if you look at the whole thing together. It may be possible to reduce EIA to almost nothing if you make the reviewable actions small enough.

Courts have generally frowned on what's called "segmentation"— where, say, a long highway project is divided into short segments and each segment is looked at individually. They've looked particularly askance at cases where a state highway agency wants to use federal funds to build a highway up to each side of an environmentally sensitive area or a historic district, and then use non-federal funds to punch through and connect the parts, claiming they don't have to do NEPA or section 106 review on the "non-federal" portion. But there are other ways to ratchet down the apparent effects of a project by dividing it up.

A good example is the mineral leasing program of the Bureau of Land Management (BLM). BLM controls the mineral estate under a great deal of federal land—not only land it administers itself, but National Forest land, land in wildlife refuges, and so on. It can lease rights to exploitable minerals, and it does. There's nothing wrong with that (unless you just don't like mineral extraction) as long as the environment is protected, but here's where BLM has developed a creative dodge.

BLM holds that conveying rights to minerals that may or may not exist has no environmental impact, because it's just a paperwork exercise. There's only an impact, the theory goes, when the lessee (the company to whom the lease is sold) gets ready to dig, blast, drill, or burrow to find or get at the mineral. At that point they need authorization from BLM, so that's the time to deal with NEPA and section 106 review.[6]

In a given year, then, in a given area, BLM may sell dozens of leases, conferring rights to thousands of acres of possible mineral lands, without considering environmental impacts or effects on historic properties. Years later, perhaps, they'll undertake review only of proposed drilling, blasting, or other ground-disturbing activities on specific sites the lessee proposes to disturb.

There are three problems with this. One is that the government makes commitments, and takes money for it, without really knowing what the impacts of fulfilling its commitments will be. If nothing else, such leases create the impression in the minds of lessees that they really will be able to extract minerals if any are there. Events are set in motion that point toward digging up an area, without any serious information on what that area may contain in the way of environmental sensitivities. This leads to the second problem. The lessees understandably invest money in exploring for and planning to exploit the minerals, and by the time they are required actually to find out what damage this will do, they're likely to be pretty committed to their plans of operation and not very flexible about finding ways to avoid or reduce impacts. The third problem is that BLM ends up examining only the impact of this little drill pad, that little mineshaft, that short stretch of access road, without ever understanding the overall impacts of *all* the pads, shafts, and roads. So we wind up with vast tracts of public land pockmarked with well pads and spiderwebbed with roads—each one surveyed for archaeological sites and endangered species, but with nary a thought for overall impacts on the environment.

Drop 'Em through the Cracks

Another way to facilitate development through division is by carefully addressing each law individually, and narrowly defining terms such as "environment" and "historic property." If you can divide the world up into enough separate pieces, each the subject of a specific law or regulation, there's lots of space between the pieces into which projects and impacts can fall.

Wild horses and burros provide a good example of this strategy. There's a specific law—the Wild, Free-Roaming Horses and Burros Act[7]— directing the Bureau of Land Management (BLM) to manage herds of such critters, which Congress in the statute found to be "living symbols of the historic and pioneer spirit of the West." But the statute gives BLM a lot of discretion in deciding how to manage the herds—so much discretion that wild horse advocates say BLM is managing many of them to death. The law doesn't provide much opportunity for concerned parties to influence BLM's management—it's largely something that BLM figures out with its wildlife biologists. So people like Kathleen Hayden of the Backcountry Horsemen of California look for ways to shoehorn themselves into BLM's deliberations, and they find NHPA.

If wild horses and burros are "living symbols of the historic and pioneer spirit of the West," surely that makes them historic properties, right? So BLM ought to comply with section 106 of NHPA and hence to consult with concerned parties like the Backcountry Horsemen, before deciding to thin, relocate, neuter, or otherwise "manage" a herd, right?

But the NHPA definition of "historic property" is "district, site, building, structure, or object included in or eligible for the National Register." Is a horse a district? No. A site? A building? A structure? An object? Well, maybe an object; one court has suggested this, with reference to another kind of critter,[8] but the National Register staff in the National Park Service has not spoken to the question. If they ever do speak, I doubt they'll speak in favor of historic animals. So when the Horsemen raise the question of the herds' historicity, BLM tends to assure the world that it's done archaeological surveys. Whatever horses and burros may be, they're certainly not archaeological sites.

What the Horsemen want, of course, is the opportunity to sit down at the table with BLM and negotiate on behalf of the horses and burros, and get a bit of respect for the significance the animals have in their—the Horsemen's—culture and history. Section 106 could give them that opportunity, but BLM can dodge it by defining the horses as non-properties. The Wild Horse and Burro Act doesn't provide for consultation with concerned parties.

What about NEPA? Well, BLM may do an environmental assessment (EA) on herd management in a given state or region, but NEPA doesn't require consultation, either—just opportunities to comment, if that. The result of all this is that there is simply no context, no forum, in which the Horsemen's concerns can be raised and addressed.

Horses, of course, are only an example. Our whole environment, our whole heritage, is fragmented by the very laws that are supposed to protect it. This is not the fault of the federal agencies, though they happily take advantage of it. Congress, and indeed the environmental and cultural resource communities, are responsible for promoting and enacting a hodge-podge of laws, each dealing with a specific aspect of the environment with little or no reference to any of the others. And most of the laws give federal agencies almost unfettered authority to interpret their responsibilities. Nobody is charged, and nothing is set up, to deal in a consultative manner with the broad range of public interests in natural and cultural heritage. So the Fish and Wildlife Service does endangered species; the Advisory Council on Historic Preservation does historic properties; BLM does wild horses and burros. Each has its own perspectives, its own definitions, its own regulations and procedures. When faced with a challenge like the heritage value of horses and burros, each agency can usually find ways to avoid acknowledging responsibility.

Like the other strategies we've discussed, ducking the responsibility for anything but narrowly defined aspects of the environment simplifies an agency's work. It allows the agency to get on with the activities it explicitly or implicitly advocates without a lot of pesky analysis and without meaningfully consulting the public. And that's what agencies very much prefer to do.

"We Don't Do NEPA on That"

The very simplest way to avoid EIA is simply to declare a project "categorically excluded" from review under NEPA. A categorical exclusion, as the term implies, is a category of action that an agency has decided has so little potential for serious impacts on the environment that it need not be subjected to EIA. The NEPA regulations allow categorical exclusions—they'd have to, or agencies would be doing NEPA analyses every time they bought paperclips. Each agency comes up with its own list of "CatExes" or "CXs"—or they may be called something else—and publishes them in their own NEPA procedures, subject to approval by the Council on Environmental Quality (CEQ).

If a project falls into a CX category, then the agency need not do an EA on it, or reach a finding of no significant impact (FONSI) or do an EIS. Being in a NEPA CX category does not exclude the project from consideration under section 106 of NHPA, or under the Endangered Species Act or another non-NEPA law, but agencies often act as though it does. They simply ignore all kinds of EIA and CRM analyses on categorically excluded actions. Most such actions really *do* have little or no potential for impact—they're things like driving vehicles from the government motor pool down the road, or hiring a new administrative assistant—so nobody worries much about them. But some CX actions are not so minor-league. Administrative actions, for example—like conveying mineral interests, in the case of BLM—may be regarded as categorical exclusions, even though they may set processes in motion that will have serious impacts over the long term. So the CEQ regulations say that in deciding whether a given project falls into a CX category, an agency must consider whether "extraordinary circumstances" exist indicating the need for more review. If so, then an EA or even an EIS may be in order.

But categorical exclusions become institutionalized. Agency people come to think of them as classes of actions on which "we don't do NEPA" or "we don't have to consider environmental impacts." And if your understanding is that you just don't have to perform an activity—especially if you perceive it to be a mere administrative nuisance—then you're unlikely to see any reason to allow for "extraordinary circumstances" under which you *should* perform it.

Translating "categorically excluded except under extraordinary circumstances" into "don't do NEPA" helps generate the impression that an agency doesn't have to "do" any of the other heritage laws, either. So the agency may not do section 106 review, or address environmental justice or religious use of the environment or water quality or sociocultural interests. This is really drawing a long bow; section 106 and most of the other non-NEPA heritage laws don't even provide for categorical exclusions, and it certainly doesn't follow that if something's categorically excluded from the application of one law, it's automatically excluded from the application of another.

Sheepishness

The Fish and Wildlife Service (FWS) recently proposed a change in the boundaries of designated bighorn sheep habitat in California. Equestrians in the area—the Backcountry Horsemen again, and others— feared this would keep them from using a historic trail. They were also concerned about the relationship between the bighorn habitat and that of wild horses and burros. There's an ongoing argument about whether these species are in conflict for use of the range. The equestrians looked for ways to influence the agency decision. They asked FWS how it was complying with NEPA. The response—very graciously rendered, I might add—was "we're not required to do NEPA on habitat designations under the Endangered Species Act (ESA)."

Why not? Because back in 1983, FWS had gotten a finding from the Council on Environmental Quality (CEQ) that "as a matter of law" such designations didn't need to be reviewed. It's not clear to me how CEQ came to this conclusion, but some time later the Tenth Circuit Court of Appeals told FWS that it *did* have to "do NEPA" on such designations. FWS's response was to do EAs on habitat designations only in the Southwest—that is, within the Tenth Circuit's jurisdiction. Everywhere else, for the last quarter-century, FWS has not bothered to consider the environmental impacts of habitat designations. It has become institutionalized that "we don't do NEPA" on habitat designations (except in the Tenth Circuit). Apparently FWS doesn't "do" section 106 of NHPA, either.

Why should they? Because while a habitat designation may be thought (at least by a biologist) to be a pretty benign federal action, it can have environmental impacts—such as, in the California case, by driving wild horses and burros out, or justifying their removal, or by prohibiting equestrians from continuing an activity that they view as part of their historic and cultural heritage. Maybe when push comes to shove the equestrians shouldn't be allowed to continue riding through sheep country, and the equines ought to be put out to pasture, but surely that should be decided through a process of objective review as provided under NEPA, and consultation as stipulated under section 106.

FWS also argued, back in 1983 (and apparently without thought about it since), that because the ESA requires that decisions about habitat and endangerment be made on biological grounds only, without consideration of social and economic factors, there's no need for them to analyze impacts on non-biological aspects of the environment. But even if biology trumps other considerations under the ESA, that doesn't mean that nothing can or should be done to mitigate the impacts of a biological decision. In the California case, for instance, we ought to find out whether there really is a conflict between sheep grazing and horseback riding. If there is, we ought to think about what can be done to alleviate the conflict without depriving either the sheep or the equestrians of their rights. Are there times of year when riding through the habitat would be OK? Or times of the day? Or are there rules that can be adopted to reduce conflict? No chasing the sheep? Put booties on your horses? I don't know what the answer might be, but if NEPA and section 106 were being complied with, alternatives would be considered and stakeholders would be consulted. They would also have opportunities for back-and-forth consultation about whether there's really conflict between grazing sheep and horses or burros in the area. Blind adherence to a 25-year-old decision not to "do NEPA" on a class of actions deprives the agency and the public —and the environment—of the thoughtful analysis necessary to resolve conflicts between competing interests. That's inconsistent with section 101 of NEPA and with responsible governance.

■ ■ ■ MALICE VERSUS IGNORANCE

I don't want to leave readers with the impression that federal agency bias in favor of development necessarily reflects malice toward heritage. Often it's more a matter of ignorance and unexamined assumptions. But the fact that agencies don't invest the money and brainpower necessary to cure the former and eliminate the latter reflects the low esteem in which federal agencies hold the EIA and CRM enterprises.

Example: I recently spent some time reviewing an "RFQ"—that's "request for quotes"—from a federal agency that will remain nameless to protect the innocent. The purpose of an RFQ is to get firms that are interested in working for an agency to state what they want the agency to pay them for a specific project or product. An RFQ is a pretty good way for an agency to procure goods and services if it knows precisely what it wants, but if there's any uncertainty about what product or what services may be involved, an RFQ is really an RFG—a request for a guess.

The agency in this example manages a lot of buildings and building complexes around the country, and many of them are old. Quite a few have been listed in the National Register. The agency is in the process of upgrading some of them to suit new and expanded functions. So it has NEPA and section 106 review responsibilities. I have no idea what the agency is doing about NEPA; the RFQ didn't say. What it said was that the agency was going to modify several buildings—the modifications ranging from replacing windows in one case to demolishing the whole structure in another—and it needed help completing section 106 review of its plans. It was clear from the thin detail provided in the RFQ that the agency was at loggerheads with the State Historic Preservation Officers (SHPOs) in whose states the buildings stood.

So what did the RFQ request? An itemized, justified price quote for providing all the assistance needed to complete section 106 review of all the projects—*within three months.*

You'll recall that section 106 review is all about consultation, and when there's an adverse effect to resolve—as there was in every case covered by the RFQ—this means trying to negotiate an agreement. The agency recognized this; the RFQ stipulated that the project would include drafting memoranda of agreement (MOAs).

Could agreement be reached in every case—or in any of them, for that matter—within three months? Maybe, but it's pretty widely known that the timing of a negotiation isn't controlled by a single party. It takes at least two to negotiate, and everyone at the table has influence on how fast the consultation proceeds—and, of course, on what its outcome may be. So in fact, the agency was asking for something that no one could honestly say they'd supply.

But that's apparently just the way the agency does business. The RFQ reflected the standard way the agency procures widgets, and compliance with section 106 was simply another widget to be procured.

So what would a company have to do if it wanted to get the contract? If it responded to the RFQ by pointing out that there is no way in the world any company could supply what the agency requested, it's very unlikely the agency would thank them and change its scope of work. More likely, it would award the contract to someone willing to lie—to say they would deliver compliance in three months. What the winning contractor would actually deliver in three months is something else again—

probably a letter saying "Dear, dear, due to circumstances beyond our control, we can't deliver, so please let's amend the contract to give us more money and time." The agency would grumble but eventually make the change, and the 106 process would stagger on toward its uncertain conclusion, coughing up federal money all the way.

Why does an agency try to procure services this way? Not out of malice; its people don't rub their hands in glee at the prospect of mucking up old buildings and wasting taxpayers' money procuring services from crooks. The agency does its procurement this way because it's what they do when they're procuring paper towels or truck parts, and nobody in their procurement office has considered that procuring soft, slippery services like those required by EIA and CRM might be different. Like every other agency, this one was treating section 106 review—and probably NEPA review, too—as a minor, bothersome, bureaucratic box to check off on the way to approving projects.

This sort of attitude makes a mockery of the laws, but it's understandable—sort of—among agencies that do, after all, have their own missions to attend to. Taking care of the human environment is marginal to the missions of most government agencies. It's made more so—as we'll see in the next chapter—by the opacity of the EIA and CRM enterprises themselves, which over the years have become ever more impenetrable by and incomprehensible to ordinary citizens and non-specialist government officials alike.

FOUR

Befuddle, Bewilder, Bog Down, Bowl Over

"It helps greatly to use . . . a term not understood."

13th-century medical code of professional ethics attributed to Arnald of Villanova (from M. Crichton, "Medical Obfuscation," New England Journal of Medicine 293 [1976]: 1257–1259)

■ ■ ■ JARGON RULES

*W*hat do you think the following means?

As an area in attainment with the National Ambient Air Quality Standards (NAAQS), Kodiak Island is classified as a class II area (ADEC 1993). Air Quality control regions are classified either as class I, II, or III to indicate the degree of air quality deterioration that the State/Federal government will allow while not exceeding NAAQS. With Kodiak being designated as a class II area, a moderate change in air quality due to industrial growth would be allowed while still maintaining air quality that meets NAAQS.[1]

How about This?

FHWA shall also conduct the Phase I and Phase II (if necessary) Archaeological Investigations of the approximately 2.5-acre Woodlawn Transfer Parcel. As above, any properties identified

> during the survey will be evaluated for listing in the NRHP.
> FHWA shall consult with the SHPO and CIN-THPO (and with
> the Trust and other appropriate landowners within the
> Woodlawn Historic Overlay District) regarding NRHP-eligibil-
> ity of archaeological properties as a result of the additional test-
> ing (as detailed in Stipulation II.B) and seek SHPO concurrence
> with Treatment Plans (as detailed in Stipulation III).[2]

The first one's about air quality, yes? And it says that the air over Kodiak
Island is—well, it doesn't say the air is anything, but it does say that somebody has classified the air in a way that makes it OK to change its quality
"moderately," whatever that means. At least I think that's what it says. And
the second one says that the Federal Highway Administration is going to
do some kind of archaeology on a parcel of land and evaluate whatever it
finds in consultation with several groups of people. If anything's eligible
for the "NRHP"—that means "National Register of Historic Places"—
they'll seek concurrence by the State Historic Preservation Officer in
plans to "treat" such eligible "archaeological properties." I know that, and
if you spend some time with the language you can figure that out, too, but
it's not easy if you don't speak the jargon.

There can be mischievous things buried in the jargon: things left
out—for instance, whose definition of "moderate" is relevant in the
Kodiak case, and how does "moderate" deterioration by that definition
affect people, animals, scenic vistas? How do the people who live on
Kodiak Island classify air quality? Has anyone asked? And isn't it interesting that FHWA will consult with a whole bunch of people about the eligibility of archaeological sites for the National Register of Historic Places,
but only seek the State Historic Preservation Officer's concurrence in
deciding how to "treat" them? And what is "treatment?" Well, "treatment,"
in section 106 jargon where archaeological sites are concerned, usually
means excavating them (archaeologically) and then destroying them Not,
perhaps, the most intuitively obvious of definitions. So does anyone but
the SHPO care how the digging's going to be done, or whether there are
alternatives to digging a site up and destroying it?

Maybe these issues are covered more thoroughly elsewhere in the
documents, but you can bet they're not covered any more clearly. Docu-

ments prepared under NEPA and section 106 tend to be turgid, convoluted, illogically organized, and laden with obscure terminology, jargon, and acronyms. It's not necessarily intentional, but the practical effect is to make such documents virtually incomprehensible to the average English-language reader.

This is more than just an annoyance. If a project proponent can make a reader's or listener's eyes glaze over, the proponent has an advantage. Public bewilderment, the befuddlement of possible opponents, works in the proponent's favor, allows him or her to get away with things that an alert, cognizant public wouldn't tolerate. They enable a proponent to impose a version of reality on the project and its effects that allows the project to slip through review without full scrutiny. It's hard to scrutinize something in a fogbank.

Obfuscation can also serve to bog things down. That's not usually an advantage for a project proponent, who typically wants to get his project underway yesterday. But selective bogging can be a useful strategy. It can keep regulatory agencies and concerned citizens busy chasing their tails and arguing with one another about trivialities while the big elements of project planning roll forward. And it can generate the impression that "the damn environmentalists" (or archaeologists, or Indians, or NIMBYs, whoever) are just trying to tie the project in knots for no good reason.

I'm making this seem like a matter of deliberate strategy, and sometimes it is, but other times it's just the natural product of a system whose purposes no one's keeping track of. Everyone winds up groping around in a fog of strange words and poorly understood concepts. But the guy with the most and best lawyers and consultants to advise him is likely to impose his definitions on the words, his interpretations on the concepts. That guy is likely to be the one with the most money, which usually means the project proponent.

■ ■ ■ BEING COMPREHENSIBLE—OR NOT

Dr. Larry Freeman, a well-known NEPA expert and trainer with the Shipley Group in Bountiful, Utah, has written a paper called "Readability and Comprehensibility as NEPA Minimums" which is posted on the Shipley web site.[3] It's a thoughtful paper that NEPA practitioners ought to read, and it points out that NEPA documents have been found inadequate by courts of law because they're "incomprehensible." Unfortunately, not many courts have done this, or have had the opportunity to do so, and Freeman seems (to me) to drop the ball at the end of his paper when he says:

> The following question is the best readability test. . . . Would a judge view your EIS/EA as a legally compliant NEPA document?

I suppose it's true in a way, but is "legal compliance" the only or main reason to be comprehensible? Are judges and lawyers the best arbiters of clear writing?

The fact is that many—maybe most—documents produced under NEPA and section 106 of NHPA are more or less incomprehensible to the ordinary educated reader. Or if they're not truly incomprehensible, they at least contain terms of art and esoteric phrases that only technical experts understand. They often twist around themselves, contradict themselves, contain trick clauses that alter a paragraph's meaning midway through. And the regulations and guidelines that people follow in writing such documents are seldom any better. I once knew a federal agency official who said he used the Form 1040 instructions of the Internal Revenue Service as his model for good regulation writing.

Some of these problems arise from simple ignorance and carelessness, and from the fact that by and large people are no longer taught to write. But the obfuscation is often very convenient for a project proponent, or for an agency that doesn't want to be bothered by the public. If they can confuse you enough, you'll give up and go away.

Substantive Obfuscation

Contorted, strange, specialized language isn't the only way to fuzz reality. One can also do it with unsubstantiated but firmly articulated statements of principle or alleged fact. In such a case, as with incomprehensible forms of expression, sometimes obfuscation results not from ill intent on the part of the obfuscator, but from simple ignorance. An agency, a project proponent, their professional staff or consultants, may honestly believe things that aren't true, and insist that everyone act on those beliefs. These beliefs and actions can generate confusion about a project's impacts and frustrate anyone who's trying to make sure they're recognized and resolved.

An example of what I think is (mostly) innocent substantive obfuscation is what's happened with the Topock Maze and the Fort Mojave Indian Tribe.

■ ■ ■ THE MAZE, THE LANDSCAPE, AND THE BORE HOLE

As you'll recall from Chapters One and Two, in the traditional beliefs of the Fort Mojave Indian Tribe, when someone dies, the soul travels through the landscape of spiky mountains[4] along both sides of the lower Colorado River on its way to the afterlife. The Topock Maze—that complex of raked gravel windrows overlooking the river on the California side—is one of the important spots the soul must visit, though it's only one, only part of the complex represented by the whole landscape.[5] In tribal tradition, the Maze and other landmarks have counterparts in the spirit world, and the soul—well, I don't know what the soul does, or even what it's supposed to do. Tribal members are pretty reticent about discussing it, and it's none of my business.

A lot of damaging stuff has happened to the Maze and its surrounding landscape over the last couple of hundred years—highways, agriculture, the railroad, all-terrain vehicles, and of course, the Pacific Gas and Electric Company's (PG&E) compressor station, gas pipeline, and pumping plant, which (after destroying parts of the Maze during construction) dumped the toxic hexavalent chromium that now requires cleanup,[6] triggering section 106 review[7] by the Bureau of Land Management (BLM). Just planning for the cleanup requires figuring out where the chromium plume is and where it's going. This involves drilling lots of wells and therefore driving drill rigs around, sometimes grading roads, and laying pipes and putting in pumps—many things that can disturb the landscape—on both the California and Arizona sides of the river. All this is troubling to the tribe, whose members would like to keep track of, and influence, where the holes get drilled.

So, if you were the BLM, what would you do about the tribe's concerns? Sit down and talk with them? Explore their concerns and discuss how to resolve them? That's probably what you'd do with your neighbors if they were concerned about your barking dog or your grapevine growing over their fence. Why not do the same thing with the tribe?

There's really no reason why not, except that the application of laws like NEPA and section 106 seems to cause people to shut down their faculties of common sense. So in the Topock case, rather than just consulting the tribe about what needed to be done, BLM decided it had to do studies to find out what effect the cleanup might have on places that were eligible for the National Register. For that, they had PG&E hire an archaeological firm to do a survey and write a report (see Chapter Two). Then they figured out how to accomplish the initial phases of cleanup—drilling wells, pumping—without running through any "archaeological sites." They presented this plan to the tribe and were rather hurt when the tribe didn't pat them on the backs and say, "Way to go!"

The tribe said that BLM was missing the point. It's the whole landscape that's significant to us, you see, not just these individual locations that the archaeologists like. And while we're not happy with all the roads, pipelines, and such that have been built through the area, they haven't yet destroyed the significance of the place in our belief system. So just missing the "archaeological sites" doesn't cut it, and it's insulting to us; it demeans our religious beliefs. We want to be consulted about the whole operation—not to stop it, but to make sure our concerns are considered, and to do what we can to keep the spiritual character of the area intact.

Well, BLM said in effect, we'll be happy to consult you about effects on places that are eligible for the National Register, and our archaeologists say that means this spot and that spot and that other spot over there. Aside from those places, there's nothing to talk about.

And around and around they went.

At one point, things came to a head over the proposal to drill a test well at a location called "Site 1" on the Arizona side of the Colorado River, to see whether the plume had gone under the river and popped up on the other side (it hadn't). There were other sites in the vicinity where drilling wouldn't have been a problem for the tribe, but the contractor doing the testing really wanted to use Site 1. The tribe pointed out that Site 1 lay within a part of the overall Topock landscape that was well documented as a tribal spiritual area. There was even a map, tacked up on the wall of BLM's offices, showing it as such. So the tribe objected, and letters flew back and forth, culminating in one from BLM's Arizona State Director[8] that was, to my mind, a masterpiece of obfuscation.

Encapsulating Obfuscation

The letter began with a solemn multi-page recitation of federal law, regulations, and guidelines, apparently designed to demonstrate that the State Director was speaking with authority and knowledge, without actually saying anything. For instance, she informed the tribe that "[c]ompliance with section 106 . . . requires that Federal agencies take into account the effects of their undertakings on historic properties." The tribe, of course, knew that and had cited section 106 in its objections. The State Director provided a verbatim quote from a bulletin of the National Register of Historic Places—*National Register Bulletin* 15. This bulletin is about how to apply the National Register's evaluation criteria. Most of the language quoted, which went on for several pages, was entirely irrelevant to the question the tribe had put forward: why BLM wouldn't recognize the significance of Site 1 to the tribe and sit down with them to negotiate where to drill.

Having fogged the atmosphere with verbiage from the *National Register Bulletin*, the State Director assured the tribe that "BLM has done this." That is, it had carried out section 106's requirements. How had it done this? By doing archaeological surveys and conducting "consultation."

The tribe, however, was well aware of what section 106 requires, and it was unsatisfied with how well BLM was meeting these requirements. That was what the tribe had complained about—that BLM was focusing too narrowly on archaeology, failing to address the tribe's broad concerns for the landscape and doing a poor job of consultation. It did not advance the conversation to say "we've complied with the law by doing what you object to." But if you say the same thing often enough, it may be that your questioner will get fed up and go away.

"Tangibility" and "Disturbance"

At the end of her recitation from the bulletin, the State Director explained that "the National Register clearly requires consideration of physical, tangible, well-defined properties." Then she turned to another *Register Bulletin*—number 38—and quoted a phrase out of context about how to be eligible for the register, a traditional cultural place must be "a tangible property—that is, a district, site, building, structure, or object."

A concept, a principle, began to emerge from the fog. There must be something about Site 1 that BLM saw as "intangible."

But Site 1 was, by definition and name, a "site." The landscape in which it lies, in National Register jargon, is a "district"—another kind of tangible property. Both the site and the landscape are pieces of real estate; one can see them, walk on them, drill holes in them. So what was "intangible?" The letter didn't say.

Instead it launched into a discussion of Site 1's "integrity." In National Register-speak, a place has "integrity" if it retains the characteristics that make it eligible for the Register. Most of the letter's discussion comprised more quotes from *National Register Bulletin* 15—as before, these were lengthy, unexceptionable, and irrelevant—but what it all came down to is that the site was "disturbed." It had been turned over and mixed up by river erosion, and fill had been dumped on it.

Being "disturbed" is a big problem for an archaeological site. To an archaeologist, if a site has been badly disturbed—all its soil strata mixed up, its artifacts moved around, whatever else is in it minced and mixed—it's not much use for research, so it's very likely lost integrity and can't be eligible for the National Register. But the tribe wasn't claiming that Site 1 was an archaeological site. It was part of a traditional cultural place, a place that played a role in the spiritual life and traditions of the tribe—and still does. To the tribe, erosion at Site 1 was a natural phenomenon that perhaps was part of, or reflected, its spiritual character. As for the fill—well, it was disrespectful, but what can you expect from white guys? It didn't make Site 1, or the landscape it was part of, any less significant to the tribe.

The Little Red Fence

The State Director threw in another rationale for not considering Site 1's cultural value. "Without clearly defined spatial limits, descriptions, and other information," she said, it is "difficult" to determine eligibility. This is a very common agency dodge when it comes to Register eligibility; I call it the Little Red Fence Dodge. If you want your place regarded as National Register-eligible, they tell you, you need to give it to us on a map with rigid boundaries drawn in—a little red fence around it.

The Site 1 case is a good example of why the Little Red Fence dodge is, in a word, silly. BLM was proposing to drill a hole in the ground, at a specific site. The site extended for some distance beyond the borders of the bore hole. The site lay within a landscape that the tribe sees as significant; the landscape naturally extends far beyond the boundaries of the site, whatever they are. *No matter where one set up the little red fence, the bore hole—the project location—would be inside it.* Boundaries were irrelevant to BLM's consideration of effects and hence to its compliance with section 106.

There's nothing in the section 106 regulations to keep BLM from simply saying, "OK, we'll regard Site 1 as part of a National Register eligible landscape. Now let's talk about the effects of drilling a hole in it and what we can do about them." So why—assuming she wasn't biased against Indians or congenitally attracted to keeping the public in the dark—was the State Director so fixated on things like boundaries and "integrity?" I think she really believed the letter she signed, and she thought it was grounded in The Law.

Let's Invent a Regulatory Constraint

Throughout her letter, the State Director kept alluding to "regulatory constraints" and "requirements." For instance, she said, without such things as a rigid boundary definition, "you (the Tribe) can see why, given

the *regulatory constraints of defining historic properties*, an agency official would find it very difficult to determine eligibility."

In other words, "Gee, Tribe, I'd love to accommodate you, but I'm constrained by those damn regulations."

In fact, the section 106 regulations—the only ones that counted in
this case—are very flexible about determining eligibility. An agency and
state or tribal historic preservation officer can decide to regard a place as
eligible for the Register based on whatever information they jolly well
please. Boundaries are *not* required. One does *not* have to agonize over
integrity. What the regulations do require, and what various official guidelines emphasize, is that consultation be done, notably with tribes. "Regulatory constraints" under section 106 are few and far between, as long as
one does a reasonable job of consultation. And, I should acknowledge, as
long as one doesn't talk with the National Park Service staff at the National
Register, who will tell you to fill out reams of documentation about the
site's boundaries, character, significance—everything but maybe its sexu-
al preferences. That's the National Register's shtick, but it's not required
for determining eligibility. Section 106 is about resolving conflicts, not
filling out paperwork.

Condensing the Fog

So the thick banks of fog that made up the State Director's letter could be
condensed down to two or three droplets. First, Site 1 was "disturbed"
from an archaeological perspective and therefore allegedly lacked
"integrity" as a tribal spiritual site. Second, the tribe hadn't said precisely
where its boundaries were, so (nonexistent) "regulatory constraints" kept
BLM from determining it eligible. And all this somehow made the site
"intangible" and hence somehow not a piece of real estate. One would,
presumably, fall into limbo if one set foot on it.

When All Else Fails, Dissemble

Perhaps feeling some small qualms about whether the State Director's letter made sense, toward its end whoever drafted it[9] bolstered the argument

by asserting that those pesky regulatory constraints "preclude evaluation of landscapes for eligibility." Now, there are two National Register bulletins on evaluating historic and cultural landscapes, and others that touch on the subject. There's a National Park Service technical bulletin on cultural landscape management, and a National Park Service program— the Historic American Landscape Survey—whose mission it is to record landscapes. Quite a number of landscapes are included in the National Register, and many more have been determined eligible. BLM itself has found ways to evaluate the eligibility of cultural landscapes—for example, Zuni Salt Lake in New Mexico and Indian Pass and the Medicine Lake Highlands in California. Did the drafter of the letter not know all this, or did he or she simply figure that the tribe didn't?

I have to wonder how much time someone—salaried by the American taxpayers—spent drafting the BLM letter. A fair amount, I imagine, finding all those bulletin quotes and carefully ignoring so much else, stringing it all together into a form that looked authoritative and knowledgeable even though it didn't make any sense and was flatly untrue. But I suppose it was worth it, because in a sense it worked. By the time the tribe received the letter, figured out that it was trash, and responded to it, the drill rig was on Site 1, boring away.

What's Obscured by the Fog

I should say that when I went on Google Earth and looked at Site 1, it looked like a mess to me—as BLM said, it had been "disturbed." But I'm an archaeologist, so that's the way I see things, and it's entirely irrelevant. It's not for me to impose my perceptions of reality on the beliefs of an Indian tribe, or of anyone else. It ought not be for BLM to do so either. The federal government ostensibly works for us, the American people, and if we think a place, a thing, even an intangibility, is important and will be messed up by government action, we ought to be able to have our say and be taken seriously.

This is not to say that we ought to prevail. On balance, maybe the best thing to do at Site 1 was to bore the hole, and in the end, it was BLM's job to decide. But surely BLM should have decided based on a full body of information about the site and the impacts of drilling. Surely that information should have included what the tribe thought, what its sensitivities were, and what alternatives its people might suggest.

But at Site 1 as in so many other cases, the decision had been made without serious tribal or public involvement, and compliance with the heritage laws was a technical afterthought—a tedious bureaucratic process to be completed with as little muss and fuss as possible. And the process was understood by BLM to be a technical one, concerned with parsing definitions and meeting rigid standards, whether they made any sense or not.

In the end, it's not clear to me whether BLM deliberately generated the fog that enshrouded the Site 1 decision or was lost in the fog itself. It was probably a bit of both.

But it's worth noting that all this confusion makes work for agency staff and consultants, who have to research the regulations and draft letters like the one from the State Director. Who knows how many meetings were held to develop the strategy behind the letter? Who knows how many drafts it went through? Lots of salaried time there, lots of support for people's careers. Generating fog requires a good deal of machinery and many people to operate it.

■ ■ ■ BEYOND THE MAZE

The case of Site 1 and the Topock Maze is merely one fairly succinct example of the fogging phenomenon, which is absolutely pervasive in the worlds of EIA and CRM. Most times, I think, agency people and consultants generate fog unconsciously, without ill intent—except for the firm belief that it's their job to advance their agency's or client's project. And often it reflects an honest muddle about what the laws and regulations actually require.

The Road to the Meetinghouse

Not long ago I was in a meeting with a client and representatives of a federal agency about a highway construction project. My client was a

"Meeting" of the Religious Society of Friends—in other words, a local Quaker group. The rather complicated project included a transfer of vacant U.S. Army land right next to the Meeting's meetinghouse—a modest nineteenth-century frame building. Use of the land to be transferred had the very real potential to block, or at least complicate, the Meeting's access to its place of congregation; it also might introduce noise that would intrude upon the traditional Quaker practice of silent worship, and interfere with the traditional view from the meetinghouse. But the federal and state agencies involved, while they had talked with the Meeting, would not recognize it as a formal consulting party under section 106, with the right to sign or not sign the memorandum of agreement (MOA) they were proposing—which didn't say a thing about impacts on the meetinghouse or what to do about them. We asked why there wasn't a role for the Meeting, why the meetinghouse wasn't addressed.

"Well," said the federal guy doing most of the talking, "the project won't have any effect on the meetinghouse."

"It won't?" we asked.

"No," he said with something of a smirk. "It won't destroy or damage it. It won't alter it in a manner inconsistent with the Secretary of the Interior's *Standards for Rehabilitation....*"

Because I know section 106 jargon, I could see what he was doing. He was reciting a section of the regulations that offers non-exclusive *examples* of adverse effect. He had convinced himself, and wanted us to believe, that only actions that clearly, obviously represented one of the examples could be classified as adverse effects. He apparently believed, and assumed we'd agree (or didn't care whether we would), that impeding a religious group's ability to use their historic place of worship isn't an adverse effect—that it doesn't diminish anything that makes the meetinghouse eligible for the National Register. Which is nonsense; if you've got a historic place of worship in active use, and you make it difficult for its users to continue worshiping there, you have certainly adversely affected its use, and its use may be the most important thing about the place. My clients politely, gently—they're Quakers, after all—pointed this out, but in the end the MOA was executed anyway.

One interesting thing about the discussion that day was that the federal official insisted on doing almost all the talking. He wanted to go through his proposed MOA point by point, explaining each stipulation even though most of them were composed of stock language pulled from an (out-of-date) ACHP pamphlet. He would cheerfully have glossed over all mention of the meetinghouse, had the Friends not drawn him up short. And—I say this based on forty years of experience writing and teaching about section 106 and MOA writing—his MOA provided no indication that he knew what he was talking about. But he could fill the air with words, and he did. His aim was clearly to stun us all into submission and get signatures on his MOA, without concern for whether it made sense or would work.

Another point of interest was that there really wasn't a great deal of substance to fight about. It would be relatively easy to guarantee the Friends access to their meetinghouse, and to arrange for landscaping to protect their view and minimize noise. There was no real objection to keeping the parcel in front of the meetinghouse in its semi-natural condition. The trouble arose from questions about how to accomplish these purposes in reliable legal instruments and from the project proponent's disinclination to address the issues at all. That preference, and the desire to ram through an agreement that reflected it, caused him to fill the air with verbal fog and waste everyone's time, in the hope, I think, of wearing everyone down to the point at which they would sign the agreement out of sheer ennui. In the end, it worked.

■ ■ ■ WHAT IT ADDS UP TO

Cases like Site 1 and the Friends' meetinghouse—only two of hundreds or thousands of similar cases going on at any given time—are examples of four related problems with the EIA and CRM systems. First, the systems have become so esoteric, involving so many fine points of interpretation and exotic uses of language, that they have become very difficult for anyone—let alone anyone not a specialist in EIA or CRM—to understand and articulate. Second, because they *are* so esoteric and complicated, it is easy to focus on fine points of language and interpretation so that the simple intent of the laws is forgotten. We wrestle over whether an effect is technically adverse, whether a given resource is technically a significant one, at the expense of simply identifying and working out the problems. We have let our analytical tools and standards run away with us and spend most of our time explaining and arguing about irrelevancies. Third, for the most part, ordinary people—and I do not mean "ordinary" in a derogatory sense—don't often have the time, patience, or specialized knowledge to deal with the technical issues that dominate our discourse. So the professionals take over and impose their own thinking and values on application of the laws. In the Site 1 case, I doubt if the BLM State Director was personally committed to a narrow-minded definition of historic property integrity or "tangibility." Some staff archaeologist, presumed to be an expert, put that language in front of her.

And finally, all this complexity and confusion can be used by a project proponent to befuddle the public, to lull regulators, to send the opposition off into frenzies of tail-chasing while project planning moves along, gathers steam, and the juggernaut of development becomes not just unstoppable but immune to thoughtful guidance.

FUZZY TERMINOLOGY

WORDS AND PHRASES USED IN EIA AND CRM THAT TEND TO BEFUDDLE REAL PEOPLE

Categorical exclusion: Under NEPA, a class of action that an agency determines has so little potential for significant environmental impact that no impact analysis is needed except in "extraordinary circumstances."

Criteria a, b, c, d: The National Register criteria, found at 36 CFR 60.4. *Criterion a* is association with significant events or patterns of events; *b* is association with significant people; *c* means having the characteristics of a type, style, or school of architecture, or being the work of a master, or having high artistic value, or being part of a significant entity, the individual parts of which may lack significance(!). *Criterion d* is for data: if a place contains significant information about the past, it can be eligible.

Criteria considerations: Conditions, also listed in the National Register regulations, under which a property that's otherwise eligible, isn't. Except there are exceptions to each consideration under which a place *is* eligible.

Criteria of Adverse Effect: Criteria set forth in the regulations under section 106 of NHPA; if a project meets any of them, it's held to have an adverse effect, and the agency has to try to negotiate a memorandum of agreement. Actually there is just a single criterion—that the project will diminish the integrity of a historic property—and a series of examples.

Eligible for the National Register: Means that a place meets the criteria published by the National Park Service that qualify it for inclusion in the National Register. Also used to refer to a place that has been formally determined to meet such criteria.

Environmental Assessment: Study performed and report prepared under NEPA to document whether a project is likely to have a significant impact on the quality of the human environment. Should lead either to doing an EIS or issuing a FONSI. Colloquially, EA.

Environmental Impact Statement: The "detailed statement" required by section 102(c) of NEPA on any "major federal action significantly affecting the quality of the human environment. Colloquially, EIS. Draft EIS = DEIS. Supplemental EIS = SEIS. Programmatic EIS = PEIS.

Finding of No Adverse Effect: Under section 106 of NHPA and its regulations, a finding made by a federal agency when its project does *not* meet the Criteria of Adverse Effect. Concludes section 106 review.

Finding of No Significant Impact: Finding made by an agency upon completing an environmental assessment under NEPA and finding that the project won't significantly affect the quality of the human environment. Colloquially, FONSI.

Integrity: A place has integrity in National Register terms if it isn't so messed up that it no longer exhibits what made it significant in the first place.

Memorandum of Agreement: Written agreement among the federal agency, State or Tribal Historic Preservation Officer, and sometimes other parties, about how the adverse effects of a project will be "resolved" or mitigated.

Mitigation: Actions taken to reduce the impacts of a project. If effects can be mitigated to an insignificant level, the agency will often issue a FONSI.

National Register: A list of historic places officially determined by the National Park Service to be significant in American history, archaeology, architecture, engineering, or culture.

Programmatic Agreement: Under section 106 of NHPA, an agreement negotiated between an agency, SHPO or multiple SHPOs, and others about how a whole program will be managed to take into account effects on historic properties.

Property: In National Register jargon, a district, site, building, structure, or object—in general, a piece of real estate, a place.

Property, Historic: A district, site, building, structure, or object included in or eligible for the National Register.

Regulation: Direction issued by a rulemaking agency—that is, one charged by a statute with the authority to do so—that has the force of law, which means it must be followed, just as a law must.

Regulatory requirement/constraint: Some aspect of a regulation that must be followed or that constrains someone's range of options.

Standards, guidelines, bulletins: Direction that *doesn't* have the force of law—such as the recommendations of an expert or jurisdictional agency like the Council on Environmental Quality. Should be followed but it's not mandatory.

Statute: Law, enacted by Congress or another legislative body.

FIVE Absent Overseers, Petty Dictators

There is no there there.

Gertrude Stein

Two federal agencies and one semi-agency oversee compliance with NEPA; these are the Council on Environmental Quality (CEQ), the Environmental Protection Agency (EPA), and the Institute for Environmental Dispute Resolution (IEDR). Two agencies have somewhat similar roles under NHPA: the Advisory Council on Historic Preservation (ACHP) with regard to section 106, and the National Park Service (NPS) for matters dealing with the National Register of Historic Places. In each state there's also, very importantly, the State Historic Preservation Officer (SHPO) who oversees many NHPA-based operations. According to the ACHP, the SHPO "reflects the interests of the State and its citizens in the preservation of their cultural heritage."[1] You might wonder—I certainly do—how a state official can reflect the interests of a whole state's citizens, even by federal dictate, but that's what the SHPO is supposed to do. There's no equivalent state position under NEPA, though state-level environmental protection agencies and natural resource departments often play roles in review under NEPA and parallel state laws.

It's these agencies that, in theory, make sure all the other agencies—the Bureau of Land Management, the Corps of Engineers, and the rest—perform their NEPA and NHPA responsibilities with honesty and honor. But if they do this job at all, they do it with great, great reluctance. This isn't necessarily a reflection on the dedication and willingness of their people—individual staff members at each of the oversight agencies often sincerely want to prevail on the federal establishment to do right by the requirements of the heritage laws. But the organization of the oversight agencies, their leadership, and the political pressures that bear on them create institutional cultures that are averse to risk and prone to pettiness.

■ ■ ■ COUNCIL ON ENVIRONMENTAL QUALITY

CEQ is the central oversight agency for NEPA; it issued the NEPA regulations,[2] continues to issue guidelines to help agencies comply with the law, participates in training, and certainly encourages honest and balanced compliance. However, CEQ—deliberately, I think—has never carved out a role in which it can routinely and systematically provide advice, resolve problems, or give concerned citizens a forum to express their views and pursue their interests. Its regulations give citizens no active roles at all; people are graciously allowed to review and comment on draft environmental impact statements (EIS), but if an agency provides only a cosmetic response to a comment, there's no penalty, and there's no one to whom a citizen can turn for help if an agency stonewalls.

It is possible to "refer" cases to CEQ before an agency makes its final project decisions,[3] but only federal agencies can do this, and it can be done only after an environmental impact statement (EIS) has been issued and approved. Since agencies are reluctant to cause trouble for sister agencies, and since strategies to avoid acknowledging serious impact usually involve environmental assessments (EAs) and findings of no significant impact (FONSIs), the allowance for referral isn't much help.

Being lodged in the Executive Office of the President gives CEQ a fair amount of authority vis-à-vis the federal establishment. It also, in theory, gives CEQ a bully pulpit from which to exhort administrations to do right by the environment. What comes with these advantages, though, is exposure to continuous high-level political pressure. One can't really buck the president when one is attached to the White House. And presidents—thus far in the late twentieth and early twenty-first centuries—have placed environmental impact assessment (EIA) and cultural resource management (CRM) pretty low on their lists of priorities.

■ ■ ■ THE ENVIRONMENTAL PROTECTION AGENCY

EPA is much bigger than CEQ, and it's an "independent" agency, not part of any executive department and not attached to the White House. But it's headed by a presidential political appointee, and as anyone knows who's tracked EPA's record during the Bush (43) years, that very severely constrains the agency's actual independence. EPA does have policing functions, but they are almost exclusively derived from the "bright green" environmental laws with their hard quantitative standards and bias toward environmental engineering. EPA can bust an agency, and agency personnel, for dumping toxics into the environment, just as it can bust a private polluter. But if the problem isn't pollutants, EPA doesn't have much to say.

In Executive Order 12898, President Bill Clinton gave EPA the role of leaning on other agencies about environmental justice. The executive order tells agencies to take steps to avoid having "disproportionately high and adverse human health or environmental effects" on "minority groups and low-income populations." Though the movement to ensure environmental justice developed because dangerous and noxious facilities kept getting sited in neighborhoods where poor people and minorities live, EPA (and CEQ, and the Department of Justice) said the executive order covered all kinds of environmental impacts—including impacts on natural and cultural heritage. For a while, EPA provided a sympathetic ear to low-income and minority communities that felt their environments were threatened by government action, and it could be quite aggressive in pushing agencies to do right by such communities. Although EPA still has an environmental justice program, it has been relatively quiescent in the Bush administration.[4]

EPA does comment on EISs,[5] and if it issues a failing grade, there are pretty serious consequences: the agency responsible for the EIS has to stop and rethink its position. But since EPA's attention is overwhelmingly focused on the subjects of the "bright green" laws, and its staff is organized accordingly, it very seldom comments on aspects of an EIS that don't involve the risk or actuality of toxifying something, or failing to clean up something already toxified. Again, if your problem isn't toxics, you're unlikely to get help from EPA.

Even where toxics are the problem, EPA is about as likely as the other oversight agencies to keep its head out of the crossfire. We discovered this (it was not a surprise) in Abó Canyon.

That Train Again

Unsatisfied with the Corps' dismissive attitude toward the 1983 train wreck site (see Chapter Three), the Rosas contacted EPA. One of EPA's jobs under the Comprehensive Environmental Response, Compensation, and Liability Act (CERCLA)—the "Superfund" law—is to identify sites that may be toxic or hazardous and figure out who should be responsible for cleaning them up. EPA will respond to citizen reports of possible dangerous or toxic sites, and that's what happened in the case of Abó Canyon. A representative of EPA came to Dripping Springs Ranch with one of their contractors, and we all traipsed up the canyon to look at the site.

It wasn't smoking, and there wasn't anything obviously noxious trickling into the water of the arroyo, but there were pieces of big machinery—they looked to me like axle and wheel parts—in the bottom of the wash and sticking out of its banks. Pretty clearly some parts of a train had indeed been buried there. Presumably they were from the 1983 derailment, and it was not certain what—besides automobiles and petroleum naphtha—might have been aboard that train. The Corps, as you'll recall from Chapter Three, had dismissed the Rosas' concerns about the matter.

So, was it something that ought to be cleaned up under the Superfund law? The EPA representatives weren't going to say, there on the arroyo bank, but they seemed impressed and said their consultant would be drafting a full report which they would share with us.

The report, when it came, was what's called a "Pre-CERCLIS Screening Assessment." CERCLIS stands for "Comprehensive Environmental Response, Compensation and Liability Information System," a database that EPA maintains of potential "Superfund" sites. If a place is entered in the CERCLIS, EPA is saying that it may have to be cleaned up under the Superfund law—not that it definitely will, or that it's definitely going to kill people or poison the local plants and animals, but that it's suspicious enough to merit further consideration. We thought that such a representation from EPA would surely help convince the Corps of Engineers that an EIS was needed before a project went forward that might disturb the site.

The core of the report we received from EPA was a checklist designed to specify whether the site met any of a series of "screening criteria." If it met any of them, then it should *not* be identified as a potential Superfund site. There were eight criteria on the checklist. One of them was marked "yes"—the site met the criterion. Therefore, presumably, it should not go on the CERCLIS, was not a possible Superfund site, was not something the Corps needed to worry about.

The question with the "yes" answer asked whether another agency was "actively involved with the site." Mere "involvement" seemed like a strange basis for excluding a site from the database; agencies are "involved" with all kinds of seriously toxified sites—railyards, old gas stations, you name it. The checklist instructions said that the reason for any "yes" answer was supposed to be explained, but no explanation was given for this one. So I went to EPA's web site and found the agency's detailed internal instructions for CERCLIS screening.[6] These instructions included a list very similar to the one in the checklist, but not identical. The "agency involvement" criterion was different. It asked if "another State or Tribal remediation program is involved *in response at a site that is in the process of final cleanup.*" In other words, EPA wasn't going to list a place for cleanup under the Superfund if the state or tribe responsible for the land was already cleaning it up. Reasonable enough, but very different from an agency just being "involved," and obviously not a criterion that applied to the Abó derailment site.

So we wrote a polite letter to EPA asking what they were talking about. And one day as I was walking home from the post office, I got a call from the EPA staffer who'd joined us at the site. We were right, she said, the checklist criterion was different from the criterion in EPA's CER-CLIS guidance.

Well, then, I asked, does that mean that the criterion on the checklist doesn't have anything to do with whether a site should go on the list? And if so, were they going to follow their own rules and apply the actual criteria their guidance said to apply? No, she said, it didn't mean that and they weren't going to do that. The checklist was the basis for deciding whether to list something, and it gave them no basis for doing so.

How can this be, I asked, since the checklist isn't consistent with your own published criteria for CERCLIS entry? Well, she said, the criteria really weren't inconsistent.

But they mean totally different things, I pointed out. Yes, she said, but they're not inconsistent.

Having worked in Washington for nearly thirty years, I know when to stop badgering a beleaguered bureaucrat, so I thanked her and rang off. What I found interesting about the conversation, beyond its implications for the Abó Canyon case, was that using criteria inconsistent with the ones EPA formally required itself to use had apparently become institutionalized within the agency and among its contractors. It apparently raised no EPA eyebrows. EPA was, and I imagine still is, systematically undercutting its own standards for Superfund eligibility.

But it worked. EPA successfully kept itself out of the argument over Abó Canyon, even that part of the argument that related directly to its statutory responsibilities. This sort of thing is the norm, I'm afraid.

■ ■ ■ INSTITUTE FOR ENVIRONMENTAL DISPUTE RESOLUTION

The IEDR is a new kid on the NEPA block. Chartered by Congress in 1998 and partly funded by the federal government, it's part of the Morris K. Udall Foundation, based in Tucson, Arizona.[7] Its job is to help disputants in environmental cases settle their differences or find someone to help them do so. This seems like a promising charter, but the IEDR will get involved in a case only if all the major disputants are willing to use its services, and can pay for them, and the disputants with which it deals are usually all government agencies, though often at different levels. It's had some impressive successes as a mediator, but it can't intervene on its own initiative, and without that ability it really couldn't provide leadership or oversight even if it were inclined to do so.

■ ■ ■ ADVISORY COUNCIL ON HISTORIC PRESERVATION

The ACHP oversees NHPA section 106 review—review of federal agency impacts on places eligible for or included in the National Register of Historic Places. It issued the section 106 regulations and has put out a good deal of guidance on how to use them. It has a staff that is ostensibly available to help both agencies and citizens use the regulatory process and resolve problems.[8] The ACHP has no real policing power, as EPA does, but it has the power to report the misdeeds of underlings to higher authorities in their agencies and to embarrass them into cleaning up their acts. And the section 106 process, uniquely among impact assessment systems in the federal government, is built around open, multi-party consultation aimed at achieving agreement—agreement, that is, on how to resolve impacts on historic places.

But the ACHP, like other oversight agencies, would much rather not get in the middle of a lot of nasty wrangling. It has designed its regulations (issued in their current form in 2004) to give itself many ways to avoid entanglement in disputes.

The regulations are set up, reasonably enough, to emphasize working things out between agencies and other parties without ACHP involvement. In theory, there are a number of points in the section 106 review process at which the ACHP *can* become involved if it wants to; but if it doesn't want to, there's nothing requiring it to do so. And the ACHP has placed strict time limits on its decision making about whether to get involved in a case, as well as definite criteria that must apply in order for it to do so.

So, suppose a federal agency wants to blow up your ancestral burial place or grandpa's log cabin or your sacred rock, and the agency isn't being very responsive to your concerns. You can contact the ACHP and ask them to intervene, participate in consultation, help you negotiate a better deal for the heritage that matters to you. And they may agree to help—unlike the IEDR, the ACHP *can* enter a case on its own initiative. But they also may very well say no because:

◈ The agency has made some key determination under the regulations, and a deadline has passed for the ACHP to object; or

◈ They don't think the threatened place is important enough; or

◈ They don't think the issues involved are interesting enough; or

◈ When it comes right down to it, they just don't want to.

The last excuse may reflect political pressure or the fear of such pressure, the priorities of the political appointees who make up the actual Advisory Council—a 20-member body that oversees the agency—the staff's workload, or the predilections and biases of the particular staff member who reviews your request. Like other agencies, the ACHP has been encouraged by the Bush administration to keep its head down and avoid causing trouble, so for the last eight years in particular, it has been pretty flaccid.

Bear in mind, too, that the ACHP can't even think about getting involved unless there's some kind of historic place known or thought likely to be threatened. It really has nothing to say about impacts on the environment that don't involve historic places, as such places are defined by the National Park Service, which maintains the National Register.

■ ■ ■ THE NATIONAL PARK SERVICE

The National Park Service (NPS) does many things, only one of which is managing national parks. One thing it does is maintain the National Register of Historic Places—ostensibly "the Nation's official list of cultural resources worthy of preservation."[9] That's a misnomer and a pretentious one at that. The Register doesn't list all types of "cultural resources," only those that fall within the statutory definition of "historic properties." And the Register isn't anything like a complete list of the nation's historic properties, either; it's a list of those that people have nominated—an enterprise requiring considerable time and trouble—and which the NPS staffers who run the Register have been gracious enough to accept. So if the kind of cultural heritage you're concerned about is, say, an animal, or a plant, or a traditional practice like fishing or cattle raising or a religious ceremony, you're not going to get any help from the Register—and therefore from the ACHP—unless you can somehow categorize the thing as a "property"—a piece of real estate. And if you can do that, you're going to have to show that it meets particular criteria, which the Register regards as highly authoritative but which are subject to much interpretation. You'll also have to show that it *doesn't* meet certain "considerations" that *disqualify* it.

An example of how the Register works, or doesn't, is what happened to the Skokomish Tribe in Washington State when they tried to protect their religious sites and practices.

Stiffing the Skokomish

The Skokomish live west of Tacoma, at the south end of Puget Sound. Much of their ancestral homeland along the north fork of the Skokomish River was flooded in the 1920s and 1930s by the Cushman Hydroelectric Project, a dam and reservoir complex. Among the places flooded were fishing sites, villages, and places where traditional dances and ceremonies were carried out as part of the tribe's religious expression.

By the 1980s, the tribe was experiencing a cultural revival and wanted to carry out its dances and rituals as close as possible to where the ancestors had performed them. They were able to establish places for such activities on the shores of the lake that had drowned their ancestral sites. But they could use them only with the by-your-leave of the City of Tacoma, which controlled the reservoir.

Then the Cushman Project came up for renewal of its license from the Federal Energy Regulatory Commission (FERC). FERC had to comply with section 106 by taking into account the effects of renewing the license on "historic properties" as defined by the National Register. The tribe entered consultation under section 106, with the hope of getting the dam torn down and the land restored. Failing that, they hoped at least to make sure that the City would respect their right to use and maintain their ritual locations along the shoreline.

The only way such locations, and the tribe's interest in them, could become a subject of discussion under section 106 was for them to be treated as historic properties—that is, eligible for the National Register. The tribe said that of course they were eligible, as part of an overall historic landscape or district that encompassed the inundated north fork and their ancestral sites, and the places to which they had relocated their traditional activities.

But the Register said no. The tribe hadn't been using the specific spots around the lake shore for fifty years or more, and to be eligible for the Register, the significance of a place must—say the Register's regulations—extend at least fifty years into the past. Never mind that the tribe had used the north fork of the Skokomish River since time immemorial; never mind that the tribe had been forced by the reservoir off their ancestral sites and up into the surrounding landscape. Never mind that they couldn't perform their rituals at the original sites without scuba gear. The specific sites weren't fifty years old, so they weren't eligible for the Register, so the consultation process under section 106 couldn't consider the tribe's desire to maintain and use them.[10]

This sort of catch-22 is typical of the Register, and it's not really the fault of the bureaucrats who run the show—though they could do better if they had the wit and initiative to do so. It wasn't meant to be, but the Register has come to be defined narrowly as a list of places—mostly buildings and archaeological sites—that professional practitioners of fields like architectural history and archaeology can appreciate. Such professionals are the people NPS hires to run the Register. Understandably, they've focused attention on what's interesting to them, what they can appreciate. They've made the Register their own, and it's become less and less relevant to anyone else, including the American public.

■ ■ ■ THE STATE HISTORIC PRESERVATION OFFICER

Each state and territory, and each of a few other entities related to the United States,[11] has a State Historic Preservation Officer (SHPO). The SHPO is a state government employee, responsible for administering the national historic preservation program in his or her state. That means nominating places to the National Register, participating in section 106 review on behalf of the state, helping local governments set up preservation programs, and performing a variety of related functions called for by

NHPA. Critically for purposes of EIA and CRM, the SHPO is supposed to advise and assist federal agencies in carrying out their section 106 work. In doing so, according to the section 106 regulations, the SHPO "reflects the interests of the State and its citizens in the preservation of their cultural heritage."[12]

So the SHPO is the one to turn to if you have a problem with the way your cultural heritage is being treated, right? Wrong.

While some SHPOs are interested in cultural heritage, most concern themselves only with historic properties. As with the National Register, if it's an old building or an archaeological site you're worried about, the SHPO will talk with you; if it's your ranching lifestyle or a fish run or your ability to carry out a religious ritual, you're likely out of luck.

And SHPOs can interpret the notion of "historic properties" very narrowly. For instance, consider the case of "Between the Rivers."

They're Not Indians

The peninsula formed by the junction of the Tennessee and Cumberland Rivers in western Kentucky was the home of a distinct set of rural communities from right after the Revolution until the early-to-mid twentieth century. They collectively identified with the area they called "Between the Rivers"; it was their ancestral turf and contained their houses, farms, churches, and burial grounds. Then they were dispossessed by the Tennessee Valley Authority, the rivers were dammed, and the land became "Land Between the Lakes National Recreation Area." It is now under the jurisdiction of the Forest Service. The Between the Rivers (BTR) families and their descendants still identify with the area and spend a good deal of time there, taking care of cemeteries and their one surviving church. They would like to have a part in planning how the Forest Service manages and interprets their homeland. The Forest Service has to comply with section 106 in doing its management planning, and the BTR people thought that participating in section 106 review would be a good way for them to protect their interests.

So the BTR people suggested that the landscape of the Land Between the Lakes was eligible for the National Register as what's called a

"traditional cultural property"[13] (TCP). A TCP is a place that's significant because some kind of community identifies with it as part of their
cultural heritage; based on that association, a TCP may be eligible for the
National Register. Quite a few Indian tribes and Native Hawaiian organizations have used the TCP notion to get their spiritual places—often
natural places like mountains, lakes, rivers, and the like—recognized as
eligible for the National Register. But the National Register bulletin that
defines TCPs makes it very clear that TCPs are not just for indigenous
people; all kinds of people can have TCPs, which may be eligible for the
Register.

But the Forest Service doesn't want to grant the BTR people a consultative role in the recreation area's planning, so they don't want the area
recognized as an eligible TCP. Behind closed doors, then, they consulted
with the Kentucky SHPO, who cannily observed that the BTR people
were not a federally recognized Indian tribe. Therefore, he said, they
couldn't have a TCP. The BTR people suggested that the SHPO familiar-
ize himself with the pertinent Register bulletin, but there's no evidence (as
far as I know) that he ever did so. The last I heard, the SHPO was saying
that if the National Register eligibility of Between the Rivers was
acknowledged, there was just no telling who else might want their traditional homelands similarly recognized. Apparently the SHPO "reflects the
interests of the . . . citizens in the preservation of their cultural heritage"
by strictly controlling whose cultural heritage is regarded as worthy of
protection—or even consideration in planning the management of federal land.

■ ■ ■ **BEYOND THE RIVERS**

This sort of narrow-mindedness and insulation from public concerns is
regrettably common among SHPOs. In the Abó Canyon case, for example, the New Mexico SHPO became fixated on the historic significance of
the early twentieth-century railroad but couldn't get her mind around the
idea that the whole pass—a major east–west travel corridor since Clovis
hunters chased mastodons through it and the hinterland of at least two
major prehistoric and early historic pueblos[14]—might be a significant

cultural landscape. In Virginia, one of the Buckland Preservation Society's frustrations has been SHPO concurrences in determinations that housing developments and road projects would have no adverse effects on the town or its battlefield, without consulting the people who live there. The Arizona and California SHPOs have participated in Bureau of Land Management determinations about the Topock Maze area under section 106, made without consulting the Fort Mojave Tribe though the actions under review were in the midst of the tribe's well-documented cultural landscape.

On the other hand, SHPOs can be junkhouse dogs when it comes to technical and procedural matters. It is widely understood in the CRM world that the SHPO dictates the standards that must be followed in carrying out work under section 106—though the SHPO actually has no such authority under NHPA. And SHPOs dictate with considerable enthusiasm. For the most part, the standards are for archaeological surveys. Here's an excerpt from one set of such standards; this one happens to be from Alabama:[15]

> Every archaeological survey must include a systematic pedestrian walk over, a visual inspection of the survey tract, and the systematic collection of significant artifacts from the ground surface. . . . Under normal field conditions, systematic subsurface testing (involving either shovel tests or auger tests of consistent width or diameter) should be conducted to the depth of the subsoil, with tests that measure no less than 30 centimeters in diameter and that are placed at intervals no greater than 30 meters (or no fewer than nine tests per hectare).

That may describe a good way to do archaeological field survey in Alabama; I don't know. The problem with these standards and their ilk—and almost every SHPO has them—is that they come to be understood as *the* way you identify archaeological sites, or historic properties, or even "cultural resources," in order to comply with federal law.

A CRM consultant recently complained to me about two adjacent states, one of whose SHPO said he had to space his archaeologists 30 meters apart while marching over the landscape looking for sites, while the other prescribed 15 meters. And the two SHPOs also had drastically different standards for what constitutes an "archaeological site" and for what's eligible for the National Register. The consultant was working on an interstate pipeline. "How am I supposed to explain to my client why costs double when we cross the state line?" he asked.

"Well," I said, "you could tell your client that what the SHPO is saying has nothing to do with any legal requirement, and suggest they go slap the SHPO around."

"I can't do that," he said; "I'll never be permitted to work in that state again."

SHPOs often issue standards for identifying historic buildings also, which tend to emphasize how many facades to photograph and how to categorize buildings as to style; these too come to be understood as gospel. What's *not* specified are things like finding and consulting local people, finding out what's important to them, looking at the landscape in general, or considering the social character of neighborhoods.

I was recently asked to help resolve a dispute over the proposed demolition of two historic buildings for a new federal facility. The buildings were undistinguished in the extreme, and nobody seemed much attached to them. But the proposed facility, it turned out, was part of a gigantic federal-state-local-private development that would transform a big chunk of the city. One might have thought that the SHPO would ask some questions about this, but he didn't; anyway, that wasn't what had hung up consultation under section 106. What had snagged it was that the SHPO wouldn't respond to the agency until it filed a particular architectural data form on each of the buildings, and the agency didn't know how to fill out the form.

Bottom line: Project proponents contracting for help in compliance with section 106 require their CRM contractor to follow "SHPO standards." These standards drive the contractor to deploy archaeologists to walk across the construction site, digging holes at specified intervals and photographing any buildings they come across. They probably pay no attention to anything beyond the parcel or alignment that will be physically disturbed, though they may photograph and fill out forms on buildings across the street. The contractor then goes back to his or her office or lab and writes a report, which the proponent or overseeing agency shares with the SHPO. Between them, they decide whether anything that's eligible for the Register might be affected by the project. If their answer is no, they're done with it; that's what goes in the agency's section 106 files and maybe in its EA or EIS. If they decide there *is* something eligible for the Register, they decide what to do about it. Usually that means digging it up if it's an archaeological site, documenting it with more photographs and maybe architectural drawings if it's a building. And the project goes ahead. Never mind that there may be visual, audible, social, traffic, and other effects beyond the project site. Never mind how the project relates to the overall pattern of cumulative effects. Never mind culturally significant landscapes or traditional cultural properties. And never mind talking with anybody but the SHPO.

Oh yes, all this is probably represented as a "cultural resources" survey and reported as such in the agency's EA or EIS, creating the impression that all kinds of "cultural resources" have been dealt with. So never mind culturally significant plants and animals, never mind culturally valued ways of life, never mind religious rituals or beliefs. Cultural heritage has been taken care of, by having some archaeologists traipse across the field and by shooting pictures of some old buildings.

This is not what the section 106 regulations call for. The regulations say to look at all kinds of effects, all kinds of properties, and to do so in consultation with interested parties. And it's even less what NEPA requires in terms of assessing effects on cultural heritage. But it's what most SHPO staff members think it's their job to insist on, and it suits the agencies and project proponents. Sure, it costs some money, and sometimes the things the SHPOs demand are stupid, but that's just the price of doing business with a bureaucracy, and it doesn't seriously get in the way of doing one's project.

So the contractors at Abó Canyon started out looking just at archaeological sites within 50 feet on each side of the railroad right-of-way, and would have left it at that—almost certainly with SHPO acquiescence—if the Rosas hadn't blown the whistle on them.

So David Blake of the Buckland Preservation Society learned that there were plans to widen a highway through the Buckland Mills Battlefield only when contract archaeological surveyors knocked on his door—

not to ask him what he knew or thought about the area or the project, but just to get permission to walk across his pasture digging holes.

So the Fort Mojave Tribe was asked by the Bureau of Land Management to consult about the impacts of the chromium cleanup on the Topock Maze, but only as the Maze had been defined by archaeologists following what they understood to be SHPO standards, under an agreement negotiated with the SHPO but not the tribe.

As long as no one challenges it, this kind of practice works well for SHPOs and project proponents alike. The project proponents follow the SHPO's rules, and the SHPO signs off on projects without exposing any politically sensitive anatomy. Who cares if it's all inconsistent with the regulations, excludes large parts of the cultural environment from consideration in EIA, and leaves many project impacts unconsidered? Most people whose cultural heritage is affected don't know enough about the law or the regulations to object to the fact that neither the SHPO nor the federal agency is doing his/her/its job.

Others

There are other agencies with oversight responsibilities in the world of EIA. The U.S. Fish and Wildlife Service and National Marine Fisheries Service oversee compliance with the Endangered Species Act. The Federal Emergency Management Agency (FEMA) oversees compliance with Executive Order 11988, which discourages construction in floodplains. These agencies have to be consulted in various ways under various regulations in the course of doing EIA, but they're not concerned with the whole human environment the way CEQ theoretically is. They don't require consultation with a whole range of interested parties the way the ACHP's regulations theoretically do. They aren't charged with looking after the environmental interests of disadvantaged populations the way EPA's environmental justice program is.

■ ■ ■ NO THERE THERE

I started this chapter with Gertrude Stein's famous comment about Oakland, California, because that's what oversight of EIA and CRM work amounts to. *Nobody* is making sure that natural and cultural heritage is thoughtfully considered in planning potentially destructive projects. *Nobody* is making sure that the public gets a fair opportunity to participate in planning, or that public concerns are thoughtfully addressed. There is, in fact, nobody in government who's even in a position to recognize that there are problems with the practices of EIA and CRM, let alone in a position to do anything about them.

Six — *All the Locked-Out People*

> ... we here highly resolve ... that government of the people, by the people, for the people, shall not perish from the earth.

> *Abraham Lincoln*[1]

> Come, let us reason together.

> *God*[2]

■ ■ ■ THE RADICAL NOTION OF CONSULTATION

A government of, by, and for the people, you'd think, would make talking with people a big part of its standard operating procedures. It would want to reason with its people about matters of mutual interest—including proposed projects that might affect people's heritage. This seems like a no-brainer, but it's remarkable how little reasoning together actually takes place in our democracy. And how little of it is even provided for in our laws, including our environmental impact assessment (EIA) and cultural resource management (CRM) laws.

The regulations for compliance with section 106 of the National Historic Preservation Act (NHPA) are among the very few federal legal directions that actually mandate reasoning together; the regulations call it *consultation* and define the word as follows:

> (f) Consultation means the process of seeking, discussing, and considering the views of other participants, and, where feasible, seeking agreement with them regarding matters arising in the section 106 process.[3]

109

Strike the "regarding matters . . . 106 process" part, and I think that's a pretty good definition of consultation in general—whether it's consultation between an agency and a member of the public, consultation among colleagues, or consultation with one's spouse. You *seek* the other person's views; you *discuss* them, you *consider* them, and all this is aimed at *seeking agreement*, though agreement isn't always going to be *feasible*.

Duh, you say. Obvious, you say. Indeed it is, but this kind of consultation, carried out in good faith and involving everyone concerned about a proposed action, is remarkably rare in the EIA game. Agencies consult *one another*—for instance, the Fish and Wildlife Service has to be consulted about impacts on endangered species—but consulting people outside government is a rarity. Except obliquely and in passing, the NEPA regulations don't call for consultation, except with agencies that have special expertise or legal responsibilities and sometimes with Indian tribes and local governments. On the whole, the public is given opportunities to *comment* on things but not to consult.

Broad-based consultation is given more attention under section 106 of NHPA—because the regulations require it, and say a lot about it—but even under section 106 agencies and project proponents often try to keep it to a minimum and focus it as narrowly as possible. Often they consult only with the State Historic Preservation Officer (SHPO) or tribal counterpart (THPO). Theoretically that's permissible under the regulations only where nobody else is interested in a project and its effects, but in practice it's often easy for an agency simply to leave everyone else out of the loop.

Consultation—real consultation—is not something that most agencies or project proponents do willingly or well. Not necessarily out of malice, but just because people aren't trained to do it, they don't think it's necessary, and they think it's a nuisance. And what's especially sad is that the people who would benefit from being properly consulted—people who want to protect some aspect of their heritage from destruction—often themselves don't push for it, don't insist on it, don't even recognize it as something that government agencies ought to do.

Why Is Consultation Important?

Imagine you're considering some major personal decision—let's say, whether to buy a new family car. How can you best make sure that the car you buy is one that your spouse will like, will be comfortable driving, will not resent your purchasing? You obviously consult about it. You *seek* your spouse's views. She wants an SUV; you want a Smart Car. You *discuss* it; "Honey, we can't afford the gas to get the SUV out of the driveway." "But sweetheart, you won't fit in a Smart Car." You *consider* each other's views, and you probably begin to work toward a compromise. You *seek agreement*, and either you reach it or you don't. If you don't, maybe you keep riding your Segway, or you get a divorce. What you *don't* do is give your spouse thirty days to comment on what kind of car he or she would like to have, and then go off and make the decision on your own. Well, maybe some people do it that way, but they probably don't stay married.

What most agencies do in the course of EIA work, however, and often try to do in CRM, is precisely that. And then they wonder, if they care, why people are unhappy with them.

In John Cleese's classic corporate training video, "Decisions, Decisions,"[4] an ersatz Queen Elizabeth I falls out of character and tells an errant office manager that "there are two dead good reasons for consultation, baby!" One of them is to get information that you wouldn't otherwise have—notably, to uncover and consider alternative ways of getting a job done. The other is that people are a lot more likely to go along with a decision if they feel like they've had a part in making it. The flip side of Her Majesty's dictum, of course, is that failure to consult leads to uninformed decisions that people don't accept. Consultation is fundamental to efficient, effective decision making, to getting things done and keeping one's backside covered; it's remarkable that people resist doing it.

How Is It Done?

There's an extensive literature on the benefits and techniques of consultation, its near-identical twin negotiation, and such variants on the theme as mediation and facilitation. Many books on the subject are popular and widely read by ordinary citizens—for example, Fisher and Ury's *Getting to Yes* and Ury's *Getting Past No.*[5] Others are more esoteric and technical. Some relate directly to EIA and other aspects of environmental policy development;[6] a few relate directly to CRM,[7] and some focus on consulting across cultural boundaries[8] or gender lines.[9]

Nicholas Dorochoff defines negotiation as "communication that allows two or more parties with differing goals to arrive at a resolution."[10] According to Roger Fisher and William Ury of the Harvard Negotiation Project, negotiation

> may be fairly judged by three criteria: it should produce a wise agreement if agreement is possible. It should be efficient. And it should improve or at least not damage the relationship between the parties.[11]

Dorochoff lays out a five-step process for negotiating toward agreement in CRM. It begins with "investigation," getting a handle on the facts of the situation, and proceeds through

◈ preparation—developing an overall strategy for approaching the negotiation;

◈ connection—engaging the parties;

◈ interaction—the process of negotiating itself; and

◈ integration—determining what's been agreed upon and putting it into a form that can be acted upon.

Such a process can't be carried forward without the will to do so. Frank Fischer, writing about the importance of bringing the public into consultation during project planning, comments:

> Collective citizen participation is seldom something that simply happens. To succeed, it often has to be organized, facilitated, and even nurtured. . . .[12]

Productive consultation has to be planned, thought out, thought *about*. But it pays off—for agencies and project proponents as well as for affected citizens. An example Fischer gives makes the case:

By setting up an open and democratic participatory process, the government (of Alberta) did the undoable: it successfully managed to site, build, and operate the single major new incineration facility in North America in more than a decade. . . . Through the process, all major stakeholders ended up preferring negotiation to conflict.[13]

▪ ▪ ▪ WHY DON'T PEOPLE DO IT?

With all the encouragement to consult, to negotiate, to work things out, it's surprising that people in EIA and CRM—and government in general—don't do it more often. Perhaps it comes from our American belief in the lone gun, the individual who makes things happen despite all the cowards and fools around him—and who, of course, *knows* what needs to happen. We grow up watching "Shane" and "High Noon" and want to be The Decider, needing and taking advice from no one.

Consultation is unnecessary, irrelevant, a mere bother if you've decided what you're going to do and aren't interested in considering alternatives. Consultation takes time, and it can be messy. A lot of the ideas that people bring forward are really stupid, and it takes great patience just to sit through them, let alone relate to them in a positive, respectful manner. And consultation is unpredictable. If you're doing it right, you don't go into it with a fixed idea of where you're going to come out. Consultation's no good if it doesn't have a chance of affecting decisions. So consulting makes it hard to schedule, budget, predict, create uncluttered Gantt charts.

Consultation isn't institutionalized in our government or corporate operations. It's given lip service, but agencies and companies seldom if ever budget for it, train their people in it, or write it into their regulations, guidelines, manuals—except by sprinkling the word around like magic pixie dust. So it comes to be something that people contracting for EIA or CRM work, or setting up offices to manage such work, don't really expect to do. They don't plan for it, they don't hire people who are good at doing it, they don't budget the time and money to do it right. Instead, they opt to do other things—often calling them consultation even though they're not.

■ ■ ■ WHAT AGENCIES DO INSTEAD

What are an agency's options for avoiding consultation? There's a rich menu of possibilities. Here are a few.

Notification

A common substitute for consultation is notification. We publish a notice and give people x days or weeks to comment, to express their views. Sometimes we publish our notice in obscure places—the *Federal Register* is a popular venue. Often we write our notices in language that nobody can decipher unless they understand our particular style manual, our acronyms, and jargon. Sometimes we're more conscientious: we send letters, create web sites, telephone people, send emails. Maybe we even meet with people during the comment period, if they want us to—though we won't negotiate. We listen (sort of), maybe even have formal "listening sessions." We hear people out (though our minds may be elsewhere). We take their input and then go make our decision—often with little or no attention to what they've told us.

Public Hearing

A popular variant on, or accompaniment to, notification is holding a public hearing. This is such a fine old American tradition that even people fighting projects pound the table and insist on it, never realizing that they're falling into a trap by not insisting on consultation instead— though in fairness, under laws like NEPA they have little legal basis for insisting on being truly consulted.

Public hearings, on the whole, are a waste of everyone's time—much like hearings in Congress. I've been in a lot of public hearings, both on the floor and at the podium, and I don't think I've ever seen one that's made any difference whatever. It's just another way of pretending to be respectful, of letting people vent, of building an administrative record, of compiling paperwork that can be ignored.

Consult Only the Anointed

Then there's consultation only with those the agency or proponent knows, whose interests are understood, who have clearly defined, more or less official roles and responsibilities—usually government officials. This may be combined with notification and even a public hearing, so it doesn't look like the public is being completely shut out. But the only ones who really have a say, who are really responded to, are the officials.

The Eighty (Plus) Million Dollar Blindfold

I was once sent to New York City by the U.S. General Services Administration (GSA) to look into how the agency was dealing with the "unexpected" discovery of what came to be known as the African Burial Ground—a place where enslaved Africans had been buried in the seventeenth and early eighteenth centuries—during construction of an office tower. I put "unexpected" in quotes because historical research done as part of the project's EIA had revealed the existence of the burial ground; it just wasn't taken seriously until archaeologists working in the shadows of the construction equipment began to find dead bodies. And then more dead bodies, and then still more.

One of the first questions I asked the GSA regional administrator was: "What sort of consultation have you had with the African-American community?"

"Well," he said, "the Mayor is black."

The mayor was, of course, an official who GSA knew needed to be consulted and whose interests GSA understood. He was interested in the economic stimulus that construction of the new building would bring, and the opportunity to clean up a somewhat distressed stretch of Broadway. He was interested in getting the best deal he could from the feds for his city. And while he and his staff may have been told about the burial ground's discovery, it had only been one small part of the complex set of issues—having to do with traffic, utility relocation, disposal of construction debris, closing streets, you name it—that are triggered by construction of a huge new building in one of the world's great cities. So the accurate answer to my question would have been "none."

Very soon, as more coffins and bodies were unearthed, word of the burial ground got out. Soon hundreds of African-American New Yorkers and their sympathizers were picketing the site. Signs went up, the media swooped in. The Internet flashed the word around the world; complaints started coming in from Africa, from people of the African diaspora in other countries. The crowds of picketers grew. The Congressional Black Caucus took up the cause. The project was halted in mid-construction, redesigned to reduce impacts on the burial ground and make room for a memorial. A hugely expensive archaeological project was carried out, including a wide range of analyses on the 400-plus bodies removed and later reburied. The last time I saw numbers, GSA's *faux pas* had cost the American taxpayer well over eighty million dollars and made GSA an acronym of contempt among many African Americans.[14]

In NEPA practice, only agencies with "jurisdiction by law or expertise" actually have to be consulted,[15] and agencies are usually happy to leave it at that, while letting the public "participate" by responding to notices, filing comments, and maybe attending public hearings. Even that kind of public involvement is really required only where an environmental impact statement (EIS) is being written. If the agency is doing only an EA, they don't really have to communicate with the public at all (though many do).

In their versions of compliance with section 106 of NHPA, it's common for agencies to consult only with SHPOs and/or THPOs and the governments of federally recognized Indian tribes if they know of any who might be concerned. There are special tricks that agencies play to keep tribal consultation at a minimum; we'll look at these at the end of this chapter.

The section 106 regulations call for consulting with people other than officialdom. In theory, anyone with an interest in the project and its impacts on historic places ought to have opportunities to negotiate. But there are lots of ways to avoid this.

Don't Ask, Don't Tell

At the very beginning of any section 106 review, the responsible agency is required by the regulations to identify "consulting parties"—those who'll be consulted as the process goes forward and may be invited to sign any memorandum of agreement that emerges from the consultation.[16] Theoretically,

> individuals and organizations with a demonstrated interest in the undertaking may participate as consulting parties due to the nature of their legal or economic relation to the undertaking or affected properties, or their concern with the undertaking's effects on historic properties . . .[17]

and

> the agency official shall identify any . . . parties entitled to be consulting parties and invite them to participate as such in the section 106 process.[18]

Agencies routinely forget or ignore this requirement, and SHPOs— who they *do* consult—often don't remind them of it. Often the "agency official" responsible for a project simply doesn't know that such a requirement exists. I once reviewed the transcripts of a series of depositions taken in connection with a very costly section 106 debacle.[19] The responsible agency official was one of those deposed; she was asked if she knew what section 106 was. "Oh yes," she said (I'm paraphrasing only a little), "that's the regulation that requires us to get the SHPO's sign-off on our projects." The deposition also revealed that she had had no serious training in section 106 compliance. The SHPO staffer who reviewed the case was also deposed, and he said that he'd spent maybe twenty minutes reviewing what the agency sent him, being (and it's true) monstrously overworked.

That kind of thing is very, very common and seldom gets held up to the light of day through litigation. So the agency doesn't bother to ask itself or anyone else who, other than the SHPO, might be interested in the project's effects on historic properties. The SHPO doesn't remind them, so no one calls the project to the attention of whatever concerned parties are out there. The (quite likely uninformed) agency and the (perhaps equally uninformed and certainly overworked) SHPO then figure out what historic properties are involved and what to do about them. By the time a concerned party—a Luis Rosas, aa Buckland Preservation Society —finds out what's going on, it's late times to be trying to influence decisions.

The skeptical reader may ask whether these concerned people can't read the newspapers, or the public notices the agency probably puts out, or the NEPA scoping documents. Sure they can, but it's a big jump from learning that a project's being planned to realizing (a) that it's going to affect some valued piece of your heritage and (b) that there's a regulatory process that may help you influence decisions about it. This is particularly so if the public notices are written in obtuse government-ese or techno-talk and published in venues that most people don't routinely read. This is why the 106 regulations place the burden on the agency to reach out— to *identify* interested parties, and get in touch with them. But if you don't want to, it's an easy responsibility to duck.

■ ■ ■ MAKE UP EXCLUSIONARY RULES

If somebody beats on the door and insists on consulting, an agency can make up regulatory prohibitions to their participation. Here's a quote from a late July 2008 email that a federal agency official sent to a group of citizens in a somewhat ambiguous situation: they were consulting with the agency on a case, but weren't formally listed as consulting parties. Now a memorandum of agreement (MOA) was being proposed, and the group had asked for the right, as a consulting party, to sign or formally object to it. I've deleted names because the case is in progress at this writing; I don't want to poison the waters unnecessarily.

> Early during the consulting parties process it was decided by the (agency) and concurred by the SHPO that the criteria for being designated a signatory to this MOA was (sic) that an agency/individual/entity must meet one of the following requirements:
>
> **1** Own or manage land directly impacted by the undertaking

2   Provide funds to implement the undertaking or stipula-
tions/mitigation contained in the MOA

3   Accept responsibility for maintenance, ownership or
operation of land or facilities proposed by this undertaking or the MOA.

4   Be or represent a Native American tribe (Nation to
Nation status).

5   Have regulatory responsibility for cultural resource protection and processes (SHPO).

Since [you] do not meet the requirements listed, we can not
include you as a signatory for this MOA.

Now as it happens, the group *does* own land that it believes will be
directly impacted by the undertaking; the agency official (without much
stated rationale) disagrees. But that nicety aside, the "criteria" that the
agency "decided" on, and the SHPO (allegedly) "concurred" in, are entirely made up. They're not derived from any law, regulation, or even guide-
line document. The agency and SHPO (taking the email at face value)
got together and decided on criteria that would exclude the would-be
signatory from participation. Having done so, the agency then cited the
criteria as the official reason it could not include the group.

In a similar way, the Forest Service insists that it cannot recognize
the Between the Rivers (BTR) people of western Kentucky as consulting
parties in review of actions at Land Between the Lakes National
Recreation Area (see Chapters One and Five). In this case it's because the
BTR people claim the right to consult based on traditional ties to the
land, and the Forest Service (with SHPO connivance) insists that only
Indian tribes can do that. There's nothing in law or regulation that says
so, but that's the Forest Service's story, and they're sticking to it.

The Corps of Engineers routinely insists that if a party seeking to
consult doesn't have "new information" to impart, there's nothing to talk
about. The notion seems to be that the Corps is infallible; there can't possibly be anything wrong with its analysis of impacts, so the only thing that
can make it useful to confer is the discovery of new, previously unconsidered data. And of course, it's the Corps that decides whether anything is
new. The district engineer, impressively togged out in desert camo, rocks

back on her bootheels or in his swivel chair and says, "I don't see any new information here," and that's that—end of conversation. Complaining that the Corps has botched an analysis is not new information; proposing that something be reconsidered is not new information. Even bringing up new information isn't new information if the Corps doesn't want to consider it so, and I can't recall an occasion, in decades of working with the Corps, when it has wanted to.

There's little or no statutory or regulatory basis for most of the rules that agencies say exclude people from consultation, but if they do it with enough solemnity, they usually get away with it.

▪ ▪ ▪ MAKE IT IMPOSSIBLE

If they can't make up a legal-seeming excuse for excluding a party from consultation, an agency can make it so difficult for that party to participate that they finally give up and go away. I was once in a meeting—about the fifteenth such meeting—on a large, complex project involving a city government, the SHPO, the ACHP, EPA, the Corps of Engineers, and three Indian tribes. The Indian tribes, as tribes often are, were made up of people who worked for a living. One of the tribal chairmen raised his hand and politely asked if it might not be possible to schedule meetings for evenings or weekends, since it was getting expensive for him and his colleagues to take time off from work to attend. The Corps of Engineers representative chairing the meeting shook her head. Sorry, she said, we're required by law to meet only during working hours.

Of course, there's no rule in the Corps or anywhere else that prohibits employees from taking part in official meetings during non-business hours. Executive Order 12898, among others, directs agencies to be flexible about such things, to accommodate low-income and minority communities (the tribes were both). I suppose the Corps representative simply didn't want to be bothered. But the tribes didn't know she was making it up, and she sounded so sincere.

Another way to make it impossible to consult is to heap time-consuming demands on the parties and hold them responsible for satisfying these demands. The agency circulates the proponent's 400-page report on its archaeological survey or biological assessment or whatever, and insists on getting comments back within thirty days. Or they insist that particular questions be responded to, in the form and format that they impose, and if a commenter doesn't comment "correctly," the comment isn't attended to.

In one well-known case in New Mexico, the Forest Service wrote to a couple of dozen Indian pueblos about the NEPA and section 106 review it was doing on a new recreation plan. The letter said that if the tribes had any "traditional cultural properties" (TCPs)—culturally important places —in the canyon to which the plan pertained, they should write back within thirty days describing the places and attaching a particular kind of map with the place boundaries marked. None of the pueblos sent in such maps, but one did send back the text of a tribal council resolution. The resolution said, in effect, "We're not going to tell you about our sacred spirit places up in that canyon, but we'll tell you that the whole canyon is really important to us. Our elders go there on the way to other worlds, and we gather piñon and juniper there for our ceremonies. We want to consult with you about your plan." The Forest Service, seeing no specific property descriptions or maps, stuck the resolution in a file and assured the SHPO that there were no TCPs in the canyon. In this case, the pueblo took them to court and forced the Forest Service to reopen the case and consult more properly,[20] but there's no way to know how often agencies have gotten away with similar outrageous demands as the price of admission to section 106 consultation, or to consideration of an impact under NEPA.

Repelling the Indians

Federal agencies have special consultative responsibilities where Indian tribes are concerned, provided such tribes are "acknowledged" or "recognized" by the federal government.[21] The U.S. Constitution, a host of laws, treaties both with particular tribes and with foreign governments, Supreme Court decisions, executive orders, and regulations collectively insist that U.S. government agencies consult with Indian tribal governments on a "government to government" basis, and exercise a "trust" responsibility to be sensitive to and try to advance tribal interests.[22] So agencies have special challenges in avoiding consultation with tribes.

But they find ways. The NEPA regulations refer obliquely to tribal consultation at various points but formally require sending documents to tribes for review only where effects on reservation lands are involved. In several iterations since the 1980s, the section 106 regulations have become steadily more directive and now are dense with instructions about consulting with tribes. In the 1990s, the Clinton administration directed all agencies to set up programs and adopt policies for tribal consultation, and most have done so. But many agencies nevertheless try to minimize tribal involvement in their decision making, including decision making about EIA and CRM matters. There are several common strategies.

Treat Them as Cultural Resources

Some agencies act as though section 106 is the only legal basis for consultation with tribes. So the agency will contact tribes, and ask them to consult, only about impacts on historic properties, even though a tribe may have considerable, justified interests in water quality, forest health, traffic, and a whole range of other issues. The agency will assign its "cultural resource" staff as liaison with tribes, expecting them to handle their liaison functions as adjuncts to their work with historic properties. This makes other elements of the agency dismiss tribal matters as "something the archaeologists and historians worry about." Letters sent to tribal governments may emphasize cultural resource issues to the exclusion of all else, and if a tribe raises issues that are not consistent with the agency's idea of what "cultural resources" are, the agency may not know how to respond—or recognize any obligation to.

Don't Treat Them as Cultural Resources

On the other hand, an agency may treat a tribe as though it were just another interest group, not only failing to recognize that tribes have special legal rights and relationships with the U.S. government, but ignoring the tribe's unique cultural heritage and practices. Tribes often have their own special ways of doing business, of negotiating. They may not be able or willing to operate on an agency's timetable. They may have to go through internal deliberations—for instance, consulting with elders or debating a tribal council resolution—before they can reach decisions. An agency simply can't hold a tribe to the same rules, expectations, and schedules it applies to other people—but some try.

Swamp Them

Most tribes—the occasional windfall from casino development notwith-standing—don't have much money, so their staffs are limited. If you burden them with enough paperwork, they may choke, and you won't hear from them any more. Since NHPA was amended in 1992 to increase tribal roles in historic preservation, quite a few tribes have set up Tribal Historic Preservation Officers (THPOs) to coordinate their participation in things like section 106 review. The most common complaint I hear from THPOs is that agencies swamp them with requests for consultation—usually in form letters with tight deadlines—with which it's impossible to keep up.

Insist That They Cough Up Special Information

The Bureau of Land Management's insistence that "Site 1" couldn't be eval-uated as eligible for the National Register without lots of information on its boundaries and character (see Chapter Four) isn't unique. Neither is the Forest Service's request for tribes to map all their traditional cultural prop-erties. Agencies insist on such information all the time, often about places that a tribe believes are spiritually sensitive, even dangerous for the wrong people to talk about. Even if the place they're asked about isn't spiritually risky, the tribe may simply have never needed to describe it in technical terms that make sense to a Euro-American agency person. When they try, they seem obtuse or evasive, and the agency gets impatient.

Often there's no real need for the information an agency seeks from a tribe. If the top of Mount Vertigo is regarded by Tribe X as a spiritual place, that may be all we need to know about it; we can go on to talk about what does and doesn't have an effect on that quality of the place. But agency people often want to apply to tribal heritage places the same stan-dards they apply to archaeological sites or old buildings. Where are they?

123

What are their boundaries? What makes them significant? Insisting on this kind of information, especially when there's no evident need for it, can so frustrate a tribe that it will stop talking and go away. Then the agency can say, "Well, we tried," and get on with its actions.

Say You'll Do It and Then Don't

Suppose the Huffenpuff Natural Gas Company (HPGas) is planning a pipeline from Los Angeles to central Oklahoma. The preferred right-of-way will cross miles of federal land, so the Bureau of Land Management (BLM) assumes "lead agency" status for all the federal agencies involved in carrying out NEPA and section 106 review. BLM directs HPGas to conduct the studies it believes are needed for compliance with the heritage laws—EIA work and CRM studies. But very likely BLM will tell HPGas and its contractors that they may *not* talk with affected Indian tribes. Why? Because tribal consultation is supposed to be done on a "government-to-government" basis, and BLM is the government, HPGas isn't. Reasonable enough, and strictly in accordance with law. But assume for the sake of argument that HPGas actually wants to do an honest job of assessing its project's likely impacts on the environment, including those aspects of the environment that are culturally important to tribes. How is it to do this without talking with the tribes? It can't; it has to rely on BLM's communication with them.

But BLM's money and staff are limited, so it's developed a routine way of contacting tribes. This varies from field office to field office, and I should acknowledge that some BLM field offices do a good job. But others just send out a "Dear Tribe" form letter or its equivalent. The letter is usually written in the most turgid of bureaucratic language. Sometimes it asks the tribe to tell BLM where all their traditional cultural places are. Other letters are more sophisticated and ask the tribe more generally about any concerns it may have.

The tribe, of course, probably isn't well staffed to deal with such inquiries (see "Swamp Them," above), so it may very well not respond. Or it may respond with its own form letter, and unfortunately a lot of these aren't very sophisticated either, just saying something like, "We have no comments, but if you find one of our ancestors' graves, stop work and call us."

BLM then happily files the response and pats itself on the back for having completed tribal consultation. Meanwhile, HPGas's contractor has archaeologists doing field surveys uninformed about the values the tribe ascribes to what they're finding (or not finding, since they haven't learned from the tribe what they ought to look for). HPGas may also have biologists doing their studies without knowing about the cultural meaning of the deer, antelope, fish, and flowers they're studying. EIA and CRM work on the project is fundamentally flawed, uninformed, as a result of BLM's technically correct but deeply misleading handling of its government-to-government consultation responsibilities.

There are obvious ways to avoid this situation. BLM could contact a tribal government, tell them what's planned, and ask if it's OK for HPGas's contractors (or whoever's doing the EIA/CRM work) to talk with the tribe, and if so, who they should talk with. Or BLM could (as some field offices have) set up overall agreements with tribes about how they'll communicate on individual projects. But these strategies require initiative, creativity, and an interest in actually achieving the purposes of EIA, CRM, and consultation. Even if those qualities aren't in short supply, there's little in any agency's EIA or CRM system to encourage their development and exercise.

■ ■ ■ What It All Comes Down To

So there are lots of ways that federal agencies and the non-governmental parties overseen by such agencies can minimize and misdirect consultation, both with the public in general and with such special stakeholders as Indian tribes. Since the agencies typically act as advocates for project proponents entrusted with analyzing the impacts of their own projects, and since they're well equipped with strategies for dodging responsibility, fuzzing the impacts they're supposed to be elucidating and generally keeping the public in the dark, it's really something of a wonder that EIA and CRM accomplish anything at all. Assuming they do.

But even if they're not consulted, or if they're consulted only grudgingly and in minimalist fashion, people still do find out about projects, and they do try to worm their ways into the decision-making process. The provisions for comment and response to comments built into the NEPA and section 106 regulations are designed to make it possible to discover errors and make mid-course corrections. How do these provisions work out? Let's see.

SEVEN

Real Men Don't Reconsider

If you can't say something nice, don't say anything at all.

My mother[1]

■ ■ ■ THANK YOU FOR YOUR COMMENTS— NOW GO AWAY

*W*hen a project proponent or an oversight agency is criticized by someone on the outside—or on the inside, for that matter—it tends not to react well. The project planning team—including its EIA and CRM components—are pretty sure they have things figured out and resist considering the ideas of others. So the typical reaction to suggestions, objections, and comments from the public and other outsiders is to reject them. Politely, of course, but reject them nonetheless. This may involve writing something that is superficially responsive to the critic's argument but in fact isn't; other times it requires burying the argument in convoluted prose, or citing marginally relevant facts or legal authorities to explain why one cannot do what the commenter suggests. Occasionally—rather commonly in the last few years—one simply makes things up to demonstrate the infeasibility, irrelevance, or plain stupidity of the outsider's suggestion.

This sort of thing happens throughout the process of EIA and CRM work, but it is most readily documented in responses to comments on draft environmental impact statements (DEISs) and environmental assessments (EAs). There is actually no regulatory requirement that agencies even seek outside comments on EAs, but in earlier, more responsible days, many agencies adopted procedures for doing so. As a result, a lot of EAs do receive public comments, but that doesn't mean those comments are attended to. The NEPA regulations require an opportunity for public comment on an EIS, but these comments are treated in the same way as those received on EAs.

Similarly in the CRM world, the consultation requirements of the National Historic Preservation Act (NHPA) would seem to require agencies to pay pretty close attention to the concerns of stakeholders, but there are many ways around this seeming requirement. In the last chapter we saw how an agency can limit the number of stakeholders it consults, often communicating only with the State Historic Preservation Officer (SHPO) and other official bodies and keeping the interested public in the dark. We also saw how, when outsiders try to get into the consultation process, an agency can invent regulatory barriers to their participation. If that doesn't work, the agency can demand written comments, often imposing tight deadlines for producing them, and then find or make up reasons to reject them.

■ ■ ■ CASE IN POINT: ABÓ PASS

Once again, Abó Pass presents an example of this strategy at work. The Corps of Engineers used it throughout the process of review under section 106 of NHPA, but that process became so contorted it would take at least a whole book this size to untangle the tale. Luckily (though not for the pass), the Bureau of Land Management (BLM) used the same approach in responding to my comments on its EA. BLM's dodges under NEPA are easier to summarize than the Corps' under section 106, and they're all documented in one letter.

Remember that the purpose of an EA is to decide whether a project is likely to "significantly affect the quality of the human environment" and hence require the detailed consideration that's supposed to be done in an EIS. Recall too that the Abó Canyon project involves major new cuts and fills to install a railroad through about three miles of desert canyon. Recall that while the Rosas still had their project web site posted, several hundred people wrote the Corps of Engineers to object to the project's impacts on cultural resources, bighorn sheep, and other aspects of the environment. Finally, recall that in a meeting on March 29, 2006, before even receiving the contractor's draft of the EA, the Corps and BLM alluded to a finding of "no significant impact" (FONSI) as a done deal (see Chapter Three).

BLM's EA came out in April 2008, in two thick volumes, one constituting the EA itself, the other made up of technical appendices. BLM solicited comments with a June deadline; I commented on June 3. At this point I was no longer under contract with the Rosas, and in fact they had asked me not to comment, since they had given up and were settling their dispute with BNSF Railroad. So I was commenting strictly as a private citizen, albeit one who knew the project and area fairly well. I won't go over all the comments and responses, some of which are fairly technical; I'll focus on those that best illustrate agency attitudes. My purpose here is not to belabor the Abó Canyon case for its own sake, but to give an example of how agencies resist thinking about criticism from the outside.

Dodging Responsibility

The EA listed its preparers, all of whom were either BNSF employees or contractors. I asked if this generated "any concern at all in BLM's mind about the objectivity and reliability of the EA's discussions and analyses," and "if not, why not?" BLM responded:

> Third party contractors frequently prepare environmental assessment documents for projects requiring BLM approval. BLM is responsible for review of contractor prepared documents to ensure that BLM's requirements and standards are met. In this case BLM's independent evaluation was performed by an interdisciplinary team of resource specialists. . . . A list of the review specialists is included in the Socorro Field Office (SFO) administrative record for this proposed action.

In other words, no, we have no concerns. We often let project proponents analyze their own impacts, but we have this interdisciplinary team that reviews what they say and makes sure it's OK. But we don't feel like we have to identify the team members in "our" EA or provide any idea of what they thought of BNSF's contractor's work. But if you'd like to come out to Socorro and dig through our files, you can find out who was on the team. And then perhaps go ask them, and maybe they'll tell you.

Dodging Full Disclosure

Back in 2006, I submitted a paper to the agencies called "Would the BNSF Second Track Project Have a Significant Impact on the Quality of the Human Environment?" The paper analyzed the likely effects of the proposed Second Track project, as I then understood them, based on measures of impact significance set forth in the NEPA regulations[2]—in other words, the measures that the Council on Environmental Quality (CEQ) thought an agency ought to consider in an EA. I didn't expect the Corps or BLM just to fall into line with my analysis, but I did think they'd be bound by fundamental principles of professional practice to note it and at least consider what I'd said. So I was (mildly) surprised to find that the EA didn't even acknowledge the existence of my analysis. It was not referenced, and no effort was made to acknowledge the points I'd raised, let alone rebut them. Or, heaven forbid, find merit in any of them. I suggested that "while one can dispute such arguments, and even reject them for cause, one cannot simply ignore their existence and hold that one is exercising professional and scientific integrity." BLM's response:

> While BLM has not addressed specifically nor incorporated by reference the comments presented in your report, nor comments by others, the EA has addressed the topics from the report and comments as they are relevant to the proposed action in various sections of the EA.... The EA has addressed relevant environmental elements and comments that express a professional disagreement with the conclusions of analysis, and to assert that the analysis is inadequate need not lead to changes in the NEPA document. (NEPA Handbook H-1790-1 Section 6.9.2.2)

In other words, "Hey, buddy, we considered your blather, but we don't have to tell you how, or why, and we concluded that you're full of bull."

This doesn't bear much resemblance to the notions of professional and scientific integrity I learned in school, but oh well. . . . They're right, of course, that asserting the inadequacy of an analysis doesn't require that it be *changed,* but is it quite proper to act as though the assertion had never been made? I don't think so.

Dodging Discord

Section 106 review had ended with the Corps, State Historic Preservation Officer (SHPO), and several pueblos executing a memorandum of agreement (MOA) about how adverse effects on historic places would be "resolved." The Rosas, their neighbor Juan Sanchez, and the National Trust for Historic Preservation, being unsatisfied with the "resolutions" (going ahead with the project subject to some archaeological data recovery and monitoring damage to rock art sites), didn't sign the MOA. Both the FONSI and the EA represented "cultural resources" as fully taken care of by virtue of the MOA's execution, saying nothing about the controversy preceding it or the refusal of some consulting parties to sign—and, of course, ignoring any cultural resources that might not be "historic properties" of the type covered by NHPA. Also unmentioned was the fact that the pueblos had signed only with the understanding that BNSF would take actions to protect the pictograph sites from vibratory and blasting effects and to ensure tribal access to the area. These actions had been agreed to only after a remarkable meeting in which the National Trust's representative, Betsy Merritt, revealed that she had discovered national BLM guidelines containing standards for allowable vibration around rock art sites which were considerably tighter than those BNSF proposed to employ. I asked if BLM didn't think that these uncertainties and controversies about effects on historic places—let alone "cultural resources"— deserved some attention in the EA. BLM's response was lengthy, but the key part of it reads:

> The administrative record does not support your statement that "other consulting parties, including the National Trust for Historic Preservation (NTHP) and local ranchers, objected to

elements of the MOA and refused to sign it based on specific identified deficiencies." The final MOA benefited from considerable input from all consulting parties including the NTHP.

And if I want to fly out to Socorro and dig through that "administrative record," I could doubtless find out what it says. Having taken part in most of the relevant meetings and drafted some of the objection letters, however, I can only say that if it doesn't reflect objections, it's far from accurate. But hey, the MOA "benefited" from everyone's input, so we all must be happy with it, right?

BLM went on at some length about how the Corps and BNSF, "individually and collectively, consulted with tribes from June of 2005 to the present" and addressed all their concerns, with the result that the tribes "signed the MOA and demonstrated their support for the 106 process." Suffice it to say that at the very least, BLM's description of its administrative record puts a simplistically positive spin on the record of a long and contentious process. As for the pueblos' support for the process's outcome —well, we'll see how supportive everyone is once the blasting begins. I have my doubts. But BLM doesn't; its invisible administrative record is apparently plastered with happy faces and convinces BLM that the project will have no significant impacts.

Dodging Acknowledgment of Controversy

The NEPA regulations say that the "degree to which the effects on the quality of the human environment are likely to be highly controversial" should be considered in an EA.[3] When the Corps put out its initial public notice on the project, several hundred people commented adversely. Many of these were doubtless responding to the web site that the Rosas had posted, alerting visitors to BNSF's likely impacts, using video that BNSF itself had produced. Be this as it may, a lot of people were concerned enough to contact the Corps, many of them calling for an EIS. The Corps, as we'll see, was not impressed. Nor was it impressed by the Rosas' vigorous objections or the concerns of the National Trust. BLM at this time was a silent partner, letting the Corps take the lead for section 106 review. Toward the end of the section 106 consultation, environmental organizations such as the Sierra Club and Wild Earth Guardians weighed in, highlighting the project's likely impacts and calling for an EIS.

The EA said nothing about any of this, thus allowing BLM to tell itself there was no controversy. I reminded them of the concerns that had actually been raised and asked for a response. Their response went like this:

> BLM sent a standard scoping letter on June 2, 2005. . . . At the end of the external scoping, our office received eighteen comments. . . . Four comments strongly opposed the proposed action. . . . Three comments did not directly state opposition of the action but had several concerns with impacts to wildlife, historic sites, scenic values, and water resources. The remaining nine comments were in support of the action to help benefit the local economy. These comments and concerns were addressed and incorporated into the EA. The final EA was made available for review to all individuals who commented on the proposed action as well as the public.
>
> According to BLM's NEPA handbook, external scoping for EAs is optional and not required.
>
> The comments adverse to the project remain limited to a small number of individuals, indicating a low level of controversy.

This, of course, doesn't respond to my question. Not only does it not tell me why BLM didn't pay attention to the objections the *Corps* received, it doesn't even acknowledge their existence. This is a fairly common ploy when multiple agencies are involved; each pays attention only to the comments that have been addressed to *it*, following *its* rules. If some poor, benighted member of the public thinks that a comment to Agency A will be read by Agency B, that's his or her tough luck. This strategy can be very effective. Not only does it confuse the public, it exhausts them, so by the time the final decision is on the table, nobody's left standing to object to it.

BLM's letter does go on to outline the comments that it had received; I haven't included all this detail because it's really beside the point. It's nice to know now what people said to the agency, but one wonders why it wasn't discussed in the EA. We're told, though, that everyone's concerns were "addressed and incorporated" in the EA; doubtless the administrative record tells us how. And we're reminded that BLM didn't really have to engage in "external scoping" at all. Apparently this reminder was to emphasize that they gave the public a comment opportunity only out of the goodness of their hearts. We ought to be grateful and not expect any indication that our comments had been taken seriously.

Dodging Consideration of Environmental Injustice

As part of their NEPA reviews, Executive Order 12898 directs agencies to try to make sure that projects they approve won't have disproportionate adverse environmental impacts on low-income populations and minorities.[4] The EA asserts that there are no minority or low-income populations in the vicinity of the Abó Canyon project. I pointed out that the ranchers in the pass are mostly Hispanic, and that the Piro-Manso Tiwa Tribe, whose members live around Las Cruces, has ancestral links to the area. Effects on the ranchers' traditional ways of life and economy, I suggested, might very well be disproportionate relative to effects on the lives and economies of other people. As for the Piro-Manso, it would be their ancestral lands that would be affected, not those of the population in general.

BLM's response goes on and on—526 words, to be exact—assuring me of BLM's devotion to "the fair treatment and meaningful involvement of all people regardless of race, color, national origin, or income with respect to the development, implementation, and enforcement of environmental laws, regulations, and policies." All very well, but the meat of the response is:

> The EA clearly defines the study area for demographic analysis to be an area within 1,500 ft of the proposed second track, an area that includes a single family, the Thompsons. . . . The demographics discussion in the EA focuses on the residents' proximity to the proposed second track in this study area and does not include the Sisneros or Sanchez families because they live 4.1 miles and 5.6 miles, respectively, from the proposed project.

And the Piro-Manso, of course, live even farther away. Never mind that the Sisneros and Sanchez families have been known to come out of their residences from time to time. Never mind that the ranchlands traversed by the project are those on which they've run their cattle for generations. Never mind that the Piro-Manso's ancestors undoubtedly lie buried in and around the canyon. In order for there to be an environmental justice issue, according to BLM's analysis, the low-income or minority population must live—as in have its abode—within the arbitrary boundaries of the study area defined by BNSF's consultants—which strangely enough excludes everyone who might have an environmental justice issue with the project.

Dodging Consideration of Toxic Possibilities

To its credit, the EA didn't completely ignore the 1983 train derailment and the possible resulting burial of toxic material in the canyon. But it reported that "only newspaper reports and anecdotal recollections are available to provide details relative to any such releases." An appendix included a number of newspaper articles on the wreck. I found it very odd that a company the size of BNSF would not have detailed records of a major train derailment and the undoubtedly expensive cleanup that followed. I asked about this, and BLM acknowledged no curiosity about the matter at all.

The EA also said that only "small amounts of metallic debris" were present in the canyon. I reminded BLM of the EPA "Pre-CERCLIS" document and sent them my own photographs of train parts in the arroyo. I asked if this raised any question about the accuracy of the EA's statement or about the thoroughness of the cleanup. BLM said:

> A third-party consultant conducted a Phase 1 Environmental Site Assessment (ESA) to identify the presence of possible hazardous material residue from a November 1983 derailment. Phase I ESA requirements for record searches include a "good faith" effort to search EPA, State . . . , local and county records. A written request for a data query regarding the train

derailment was submitted to the New Mexico Environmental Department. As a resultant of their expansive data search, they were unable to find any information regarding the incident.

As far as I can tell, the "third-party consultant" was a consultant for BNSF, and apparently the consultant didn't search BNSF's records, instead just sending a query to the New Mexico Environment Department, which BLM says—on the basis of what data, we're not told—conducted an "expansive data search." Well, maybe.

BLM went on to tell me that BNSF's contractor had gotten information from news accounts—I knew that, thank you—and that "the proposed route of Alternative E (Proposed Action) does not travel near the area of the 1983 derailment." I guess it depends on what you call "near"; Alternative E would be in a new cut on the other side of the existing tracks from where the train parts are evidently buried; another alternative appears on the EA's maps to pass right through the site. In any event,

> The nature of the cleanup efforts have been adequately demonstrated through field visits with agencies and documentation in the administrative record. However, as a precautionary measure, the EA states . . . that BNSF would conduct Environmental Construction Monitoring (ECM) during construction activities closest to the vicinity of the 1983 derailment to reduce the risk of inadvertently disturbing unknown hazardous materials to the extent practicable.

The question of whether under EPA rules the Pre-CERCLIS checklist indicated that the site should be identified as a hazardous one (see Chapter Five) seems to have gone right over BLM's head. BLM responded to my submission of the checklist document by summarizing its contents for me and then focusing on the derailed car that carried petroleum naphtha.

> Petroleum naphtha is a highly flammable liquid and is not a chemical regulated by CERCLA.

Right, but that's not the point. The naphtha burned up, but it's what *else* might have been on the train that's of interest. To me, that is; apparently it's not interesting enough to BLM to make it want to find out.

Dodging Alternatives Analysis

The EA never mentioned the Nemati tunnels, at least by name, and Dr. Nemati's report wasn't included in the bibliography. Again, as BLM told the story, the argument over tunnel alternatives had never occurred. There was only a brief allusion to "additional routes proposed by a local landowner." I commented:

> This is a bit disingenuous. In fact, the "additional routes"—tunnels that would substantially or entirely remove the railroad from the canyon, arguably producing operational efficiencies and a higher level of safety and security from terrorist attack than any of the at-grade alternatives, were not proposed by "a local landowner" but by Dr. Kamran Nemati, an internationally known engineer, in a report that the EA fails to cite. This report is provided as Attachment 4 to these comments. Dr. Nemati's proposal was challenged in a document prepared for BNSF by Robert J. Boileau, whose argument was rebutted in a meeting with Corps and BNSF personnel on June 16, 2006 by another highly qualified engineer, Gordon Clarke (Dr. Nemati being out of the country). Only what appears to be a version of Mr. Boileau's arguments is included in the EA and its appendices. Does BLM believe that decision makers and the public are given a balanced evaluation of alternatives when an environmental assessment contains only one side of an engineering argument? Does BLM believe that representing only one side of such an argument reflects professional and scientific integrity? Does BLM intend to provide a further consideration of the Nemati tunnel alternatives that takes views other than BNSF's into account?

BLM replied:

> Mr. Clarke rebutted Mr. Boileau's verified statement at a June 16, 2006 meeting at the Corps. Sarah Naranjo and Brian Bellew of the BLM attended this meeting at the Corps regarding the feasibility and potential impacts from the Nemati tunnel alternatives. At this meeting, the Corps attempted to ascertain how

> the Nemati tunnel alternatives differed from the tunnel alternative under consideration as one of the potential BNSF alignments. Mr. Clarke indicated these tunnel alternatives were designed over a weekend and not subject to extensive engineering considerations, such as the feasibility of their locations in geologically unstable landslide areas.

It's hard to comment on this one without being snide. "Attempted to ascertain how the Nemati alternatives differed" from those considered by BNSF? A good start at this attempt might have been to read Dr. Nemati's report, which went into considerable detail about his alternatives as distinguished from those considered by the railroad. "Designed over a weekend?" Dr. Nemati spent several days in the field and some weeks working on his report. "Not subject to extensive engineering considerations?" It was those extensive engineering considerations that we had tried to get the agencies to develop, through preparation of an EIS.

> Further questioning of Mr. Clarke by Corps personnel demonstrated the potential adverse effects from the Nemati tunnel alternatives did not differ substantially from the other alignments under consideration, particularly concerning matters of vibratory effects, tunnel portals, and waste materials (from a tunnel-boring machine).

So a tunnel bored completely under the pass has environmental impacts equivalent to blasting cuts through and piling rock in the canyon and its surroundings? It would be interesting to see some data-based rationale for this proposition, perhaps in the EA, but

> As demonstrated in the administrative record, the Corps' and BLM's conclusions from this meeting and subsequent review by internal experts were that the Nemati tunnel alternatives' cost, effects, and design were sufficiently similar to an existing tunnel alternative, previously subject to more rigorous engineering. The document explained why this alternative was eliminated from detailed analysis in accordance with the 40 CFR 1502.14.

Again the administrative record saves the day. By the way, 40 CFR 1502.14, part of the CEQ NEPA regulations, requires among other things that agencies:

(a) Rigorously explore and objectively evaluate all reasonable alternatives, and for alternatives which were eliminated from detailed study, briefly discuss the reasons for their having been eliminated.

(b) Devote substantial treatment to each alternative considered in detail, including the proposed action so that reviewers may evaluate their comparative merits.

BLM's response is an example of simply making up an excuse for rejecting a commenter's objection—to say nothing of rejecting an alternative developed by a prominent expert. By not acknowledging the existence of Dr. Nemati's report,[5] and rigorously resisting comprehension or discussion of how his proposals differed from the much smaller-scale tunneling[6] BNSF had considered, BLM creates a world in which all the "reasonable" alternatives have been considered, and the Nemati alternative doesn't even need to be discussed.

Dodging Admitting Uncertainty

According to the NEPA regulations, one reason for doing an EIS is to explore uncertainties about environmental impacts.[7] During section 106 review, there had been much argument about how blasting would affect nearby pictographs on the canyon walls. BNSF's consultants had argued that the fractured sandstone of the area "would behave similarly to mass concrete" and hence could be shaken up at 12 inches per second without damage to the paintings. The National Trust for Historic Preservation had pointed out that BLM standards for geophysical exploration[8] set a standard of no more than 0.75 inches per second in the vicinity of rock art, and asked why that standard hadn't been employed. BNSF and the Corps had provided no answer to this other than that they would monitor blasting to keep any damage from occurring.[9] This would, of course, be a neat trick, since by the time a monitor noticed that the paintings were falling off the walls—well, you get the picture.

Eventually the Corps and BNSF agreed with the concerned pueblos to conduct monitored testing at some distance from the rock art first, and then adjust their methodology based on the results. This was an improvement, though it would have been nice to resolve the question of blasting effects before a decision was made to let the project go forward, rather than after.

The EA repeated the "mass concrete" business and outlined the monitoring program. I asked if the history of the debate and the existence of the monitoring program didn't suggest uncertainty about what the blasting would actually do, and whether this, combined with the pueblos' serious concern, didn't argue for doing an EIS. BLM responded by reciting the goals and methods of the monitoring program and telling me that

> The BLM asserts that adequate measures have been put in place to protect the rock art sites.

So, from BLM's perspective, there's no uncertainty about the fate of the rock art, despite the fact that a monitoring program has been put in place to resolve that uncertainty.

■ ■ ■ WELL . . .

I could go on and on. I did go on and on in my letter to BLM, and they did the same back to me, about endangered species, cumulative effects, and other issues, but this chapter is long enough, I think, to convey the flavor of how agencies dodge serious consideration of outside concerns. They obfuscate, they ignore things, they recast history, they assert that all is answered in largely inaccessible "administrative records," and when worse comes to worst, they simply invent something.

The Abó Pass case is not unique or even unusual, but it illustrates just how far EIA and CRM analyses have drifted from the model of objective analysis—how much they have become merely expensive apologetics for decisions that for all practical purposes have been made before the studies even get underway.

EIGHT

Doing Something about It

I will restore scientific integrity and the public interest to the management of federal lands.

Barack Obama[1]

▪ ▪ ▪ SO WHAT'S THE PROBLEM?

*T*o summarize: At least five things are wrong with environmental impact assessment (EIA) and cultural resource management (CRM) practice in the United States (and elsewhere).

1 The specialist firms that perform EIA and CRM view themselves as members of their clients' planning teams, and behave accordingly. Their clients usually are the proponents of the actions whose impacts they are studying. Their analyses, reports, and interactions with other stakeholders are inevitably shaped by their relationships with their clients.

2 It might nevertheless be possible to obtain honest analyses of project impacts on our natural and cultural heritage if the federal agencies responsible for complying with the National Environmental Policy Act (NEPA) and section 106 of the National Historic Preservation Act (NHPA) took their responsibilities seriously, but they don't. On the whole, they regard EIA and CRM as processes of getting and giving "clearance" to projects, and they seek to do so with as little impediment as possible to the interests of project proponents.

3 We might *still* have tolerable EIA and CRM systems if there were strong, enlightened oversight by agencies like the Council on Environmental Quality (CEQ) and the Advisory Council on Historic Preservation (ACHP) basing their oversight on principles like those in section 101 of NEPA—but there is not. CEQ and ACHP are compromised structurally and politically, and they have no real authority. If they ever provided serious oversight, they do so no longer. Oversight agencies that do exercise a degree of authority, like State Historic Preservation Officers (SHPOs), tend to propound on and belabor technical fine points at the expense of policy and principle.

4 We might still at least *sometimes* see EIA and CRM results we could believe in if there were transparency in the review systems, with serious opportunities for stakeholders besides proponents and agencies to participate in and influence project review. But the systems are not transparent, and the limited opportunities for participation that do exist often are illusory.

5 But we have all pretty much accepted the fact that this is the way things are, and we resist even considering change.

Why don't we do something about this? There are two reasons.

■ ■ ■ VESTED INTERESTS AND FEAR OF FLYING

Among professionals in EIA and CRM, there is something akin to contentment with things as they are. Yeah, what we do isn't always much fun, and no, it doesn't necessarily accomplish much. But hell, it beats flipping burgers or working in a bank, and there aren't enough academic jobs to go around. We're doing all right ourselves, and we need to keep our jobs, so we're just going to keep on keepin' on. Please don't rock our boat.

Among people who want to save some aspect or aspects of their heritage, I find a lot of discontent, in some cases cynicism, but not much organized effort to find solutions. There's a well institutionalized fear in the conservation/preservation world that if we "open up" laws like NEPA and NHPA to change, the changes we'll get will not be ones we like. Based on the experience of the last eight years, this fear is not groundless, but interestingly, I heard it expressed almost as often during the Clinton administration as I have since the Bush ascendance. I could attribute it to a Republican-dominated Congress, but I've heard it, really, for as long as I've been around Washington—some thirty years now.

So most of us muddle along doing what we do, content with or at least resigned to the status quo. Or we rail about how impure and pointless EIA and CRM are, but shrink from taking steps to make them better.

These are understandable ways of thinking and living, but in the long run I don't think they're tenable. If EIA isn't reliably producing responsible assessments of environmental impacts, if CRM doesn't manage cultural resources in the public interest, it's hard to believe the public will forever keep funding them and putting up with them. In our own self-interest, if we're EIA and CRM practitioners, we need to clean up our act. And if we're people who'd like to keep our heritage, we really ought to try to fix the systems that are supposed to give it a fighting chance at survival.

But how?

▪ ▪ ▪ CALDWELL'S PRESCRIPTIONS

In concluding his 1998 retrospective analysis and critique of NEPA, the late Lynton K. Caldwell listed seven ways that the law could be strengthened.[2] With a little tweaking, the list can be made to apply to NHPA as well, and it's a good list—though not, I think, quite realistic or complete.

Caldwell's seven "alternatives to strengthen NEPA" are:

1   Enlarge public understanding of the need for an effective environmental policy, which is also policy for people in relation to the environment, and the importance of NEPA principles for America's future.

2   Ensure that the importance of NEPA principles are present in the attention span of political party leaders and the shapers of public opinion.

3   Provide institutional nonjudicial means for the appropriate resolution or mediation of conflicts over issues of environmental quality.

4   Reform the committee structure of the Congress to provide for a more responsible consideration of environmental issues and possibly to establish a Joint House-Senate Committee on the Environment.

5   Revise NEPA to clarify and strengthen its statutory provisions.

6   Restore the Council on Environmental Quality to its intended role in the Executive Office of the President as provided by Title II of NEPA.

7   Amend the U.S. Constitution to give environmental protection the status of fundamental law.

Caldwell went on to discuss each of these non-exclusive "alternatives" in some detail.[3] In this chapter I'd like to reflect on each of them in the light of what we've gone over in the preceding chapters. I'll suggest some adjustments and consider how Caldwell's prescriptions, or variants on them, might be made to happen. Or not.

Enlarging Public Understanding

It's notable that Caldwell's book, like Lindstrom and Smith's similar critique of NEPA three years later, seems to have sunk like a stone. Certainly none of its recommendations have been implemented, or even—as far as I can tell—very seriously considered. Much of this doubtless reflects poor timing. Recommendations like Caldwell's were at best irrelevant to the administration and Congress that took office in 2000. But a big part of the problem, I think, lies in a lack of public attention to, or even knowledge of, the NEPA review process. Beyond the vague notion that government requires environmental impact statements for some reason, most people don't know NEPA exists, much less that there's a problem with it. So enlarging public understanding of the process is a good idea, but before we can do that, we need to know why the public doesn't understand in the first place. And this, I think, results largely from the character of the process itself, as it sprang from the statute and has evolved over the years.

NEPA is not a public-friendly statute. It was a product of what Frank Fischer[4] has called the "Age of Expertise," in which expert analysis was trusted to provide solutions—mostly technological ones—to society's problems. Oddly, this trust in expertise seems to have developed coincidentally with the great social movements toward equality and civil rights. Perhaps the experts took over issues like environmental protection while the rest of society's attention was engaged elsewhere.

Whatever its social history, the expert-oriented culture out of which NEPA grew assigns the public a passive role. Decisions are to be made based on the best available information—particularly scientific analyses where environmental decisions are concerned—as interpreted for decision makers by experts. The public is to be kept informed, to have opportunities for input, but it is not actually engaged in the decision-making process except through its elected representatives in government.

Reflecting this philosophy, the NEPA regulations permit an agency to *seek public input* when developing the scope of an environmental impact statement (EIS)—though they do not require it. And they require that the public have the *opportunity to comment* on EISs in draft.[5] That's it, and in Chapter Seven we saw what kind of response a member of the public's comments are likely to get. With such comment-and-response as the major interface between the public and NEPA, it is hardly a surprise that we have yet to see a vigorous "friends of NEPA" movement. Most people— even people who want to save the environment—don't have much investment in NEPA.

Thanks to the populist leanings of its primary creator, the late Robert R. Garvey, Jr., section 106 of NHPA has regulations[6] that insist on actual *consultation* with the interested public, aimed at reaching binding agreements. NEPA requires only consultation with government agencies that have "jurisdiction by law or expertise." As we've seen, agencies and project proponents find ways to ignore, sidestep, and otherwise vitiate the section 106 consultation process, and the process has evolved into one that is anything but easy for a nonspecialist to break into. The fact remains, however, that concerned members of the public have a fighting chance to get directly involved in section 106 review, and no chance at all to be seriously included in deliberations under NEPA.

The expert-focused, science-based character of NEPA works against public involvement in a more intrinsic way, too. Not to put too fine a point on it, experts and scientists tend to be liberal in their political views, while a large percentage of the American electorate classifies itself as conservative. Conservatives are not necessarily anti-environment, but they are protective of such institutions as private property rights and the right to bear arms. To the extent that NEPA and the impact assessment activities it promotes are seen as something that pointy-headed liberal scientists impose to restrict individual rights, the more conservative segments of the public will be cool to them.

But protecting heritage, and giving citizens a fair shot at saving what's dear to them, are not exclusively liberal values; many conservatives would argue quite the opposite. The use of laws like NEPA and NHPA to fend off the excesses of the federal government is something that some conservatives support with enthusiasm. The Rosas in New Mexico and the members of the Buckland Preservation Society in Virginia are private property owners who may or may not classify themselves as conservatives, but they are certainly not traditional liberals. The members of the Backcountry Horsemen of California who correspond with me about protecting wild horse and burro herds are mostly conservative and proud of it. Where laws like NEPA and NHPA are understood (as I think they should be) as means of protecting the heritage of ordinary Americans from the depredations and mindlessness of federal agencies and big corporations, I've found that they resonate pretty well with conservatives.

To enlarge public understanding of NEPA, then, I think it's necessary to restructure the review process so that it engages the public and respects the heritage interests of individuals in the ways that section 106 (in theory) does—though without all the twists, turns, and catch-22s that have come to characterize section 106 consultation as it has evolved. I'll return to this idea a bit later.

Of course, Caldwell had in mind more than the project review process when he called for building public understanding; indeed, he may not have really been thinking about the review process at all. What troubled Caldwell was that the government had never really taken seriously the policies laid out in section 101 of NEPA. It was these policies that he wanted the public to understand, and force its elected representatives to embrace. That's a worthy goal, and it's probably impossible to integrate wise management of the environment into government decisions without achieving it. But I don't think most people relate very comfortably to the abstractions of public policy. People react to situations and events, and become involved in them, when those things somehow affect them. NEPA needs to be a tool that people—people with all levels and kinds of expertise and of all political persuasions—can use to influence government decisions that affect them; otherwise NEPA's policies will never be anything but abstractions.

Political Leadership

When Caldwell called on us to "[e]nsure that the importance of NEPA principles are present in the attention span of political party leaders and the shapers of public opinion," he meant that we should "[e]lect . . . an environmentally concerned Congress and president," by "keeping environmental protection in the forefront of political party agendas."[7] He recognized that this couldn't be done without an engaged public, so this "alternative" is really only one means of putting increased public understanding to work.

Caldwell mentions as a matter of common knowledge—and it is—that "the conservative wing of the Republican Party . . . has been hostile to environmental legislation and to NEPA in particular."[8] This brings us back to the problematical fact that laws like NEPA are perceived by many conservatives to be the darlings of left-leaning scientists.

In 2005, conservative Republican members of the House of Representatives—then firmly under their party's control—launched attacks on both NEPA and section 106 of NHPA. The usual suspects—environmental organizations, the National Trust for Historic Preservation—sprang to the statutes' defense, provoking yawns from the congressmen spearheading the attack. What must have been confusing to those conservative leaders, though, was that they simultaneously began to be urged by some of their conservative constituents to *strengthen* section 106. These voters liked section 106 and wanted it made stronger because it gave them some protection—though not enough—from arrogant federal land management agencies that threatened their traditional ways of life on the land. I don't know how much this took the wind out of any of the reformers' sails—the whole business blew over with no changes made in the laws—but it suggested to me that it's possible to build support for the heritage laws, and elect supporters of the laws to Congress, without somehow transforming the electorate into a majority liberal population. But building such support, I think, depends on making the laws more open than they now are to meaningful citizen participation, and more respectful than they sometimes now are toward things like traditional land uses and the interests of hunters, herders, and property owners.

Mediation

When Caldwell wrote his book, the Institute for Environmental Dispute Resolution (IEDR)[9] had just been created, and he held out hope that it would do some good. IEDR has had some impressive successes, but as presently constituted, its influence is limited at best.

In late 2007, as the Abó Pass case entered its endgame, the Council on Environmental Quality (CEQ) published *A Citizen's Guide to the NEPA*.[10] In a section on "who oversees the NEPA process," the Guide outlined the roles of CEQ itself and of the Environmental Protection Agency (EPA), and then turned to the IEDR. The IEDR, it said,

> provides an independent, neutral, place for Federal agencies to work with citizens as well as State, local, and tribal governments, private organizations and businesses to reach common ground.[11]

That looked pretty encouraging, so I dashed off an email to the IEDR, asking what it would take to get them involved in our case. I soon found myself on the phone with a very congenial EIDR representative, who explained that most of their mediation takes place between agencies, or between a federal agency and a state, local, or tribal government. They couldn't intervene without an invitation by such a party and the acquiescence of the relevant federal agency, and of course they had to be paid.

This was pretty much what I'd expected, and of course it was a dead end for Abó Pass; neither the Corps nor BLM was likely to agree to mediation. They had no reason to; they were winning, and the Rosas—mere citizen landowners—had no power. The requirement for all sides of a dispute to agree to mediation, and usually share costs, is quite common in mediation practice, and understandable; if the parties aren't willing to cooperate, mediation isn't likely to do any good. But the IEDR's laudable adherence to mediation principles means that it's useless in situations where federal agencies are manipulating the environmental review process for their own ends or for those of project proponents. The IEDR is a good idea, and potentially an important institution, but it can't do much to improve NEPA practice if it lacks the ability (to say nothing of the desire) to force its way into a case on its own initiative, or at the request of a non-agency.

Here again, the section 106 process provides something of a model—not a model that works very well, but a model in principle nonetheless. At a number of points in section 106 review, the Advisory Council on Historic Preservation can involve itself in a case and work with the other involved parties toward a resolution. This is not exactly mediation. Strictly speaking, mediation is a voluntary process, and agencies seldom volunteer to have the Advisory Council come in and ask embarrassing questions. I suppose it might better be called "facilitation"; when I worked for the Council we called it "beating up on the agencies." It's by no means a perfect arrangement, if for no other reason than that the Council is itself a government agency, subject to the same influences as any other such agency, but it allows the Advisory Council, if it wishes, to be a little less wimpy than the IEDR has to be.

Reform the Congressional Committee Structure

Caldwell served as a consultant to the U.S. Senate Committee on Interior and Insular Affairs during the run-up to NEPA's enactment. It was in this role that he effectively invented the NEPA review process. So he naturally and rightly emphasized the importance of somehow restructuring the committees and subcommittees that construct and process legislation, to make them more knowledgeable about and responsive to environmental concerns. It's a great idea, but like his "leadership" alternative, it requires an informed and activist public—or a dedicated, influential, and political-ly astute senator or congressman in the mold of the late Senator Henry M. ("Scoop") Jackson (D-WA), who was largely responsible for enactment of both NEPA and NHPA.

Since Caldwell's book was published, there have been changes in the committee structures of both the House and Senate, but they haven't had a salutary effect on practice under the heritage laws—or on the practices of Congress, for that matter. The committees and subcommittees that busy themselves with environmental, cultural resource, and land-use leg-islation have shown no more enlightenment or initiative than the rest of the Congress, which the polls tell us now garners even less public respect than the Bush administration has.

Revise NEPA

Caldwell's legislative alternative—fixing the statute itself—was directed primarily to putting teeth in section 101, to make NEPA's policy actually mean something. He's not very explicit about how legislation could do this.

The policies laid out in section 101 are hortatory—they call on gov-ernment to Do Good Things:

◈ use all practicable means and measures . . . to foster and pro-mote the general welfare, to create and maintain conditions under which man and nature can exist in productive harmo-ny, and fulfill the social, economic, and other requirements of present and future generations of Americans[12]

◈ fulfill the responsibilities of each generation as trustee of the environment for succeeding generations[13]

◈ assure for all Americans safe, healthful, productive, and esthetically and culturally pleasing surroundings[14]

◈ attain the widest range of beneficial uses of the environment without degradation[15]

◈ preserve important historic, cultural, and natural aspects of our national heritage[16]

◈ maintain, wherever possible, an environment which supports diversity and variety of individual choice[17]

◈ achieve a balance between population and resource use.[18]

◈ enhance the quality of renewable resources[19]

◈ approach the maximum attainable recycling of depletable resources.[20]

All fine things to call for, things that government ought to do, but how can they be translated into directions that a government agency will actually follow? The history of the National Historic Preservation Act (NHPA) provides a cautionary lesson.

In 1980, under the leadership of the late Congressman John Seiberling (D-OH), Congress amended NHPA in a variety of ways. One amendment added national policies as section 2 of the statute, modeled on those in NEPA section 101.[21] Another—probably reflecting recognition that NEPA's policies were mostly ignored—added a new section 110(d), saying:

> Consistent with the agency's mission and mandates, all Federal agencies shall carry out agency programs and projects (including those under which any Federal assistance is provided or any Federal license, permit, or other approval is required) in accordance with the purposes of this Act and give consideration to programs and projects which will further the purposes of this Act.[22]

So, since 1980, NHPA has laid out policies similar to NEPA's, and—unlike NEPA—has told agencies quite explicitly that they have to follow them. But NHPA's policies are no better adhered to today than are NEPA's. In my experience, most CRM practitioners don't know what section 110(d) requires, and don't know what section 2 says. Some agency guidelines give lip service to NHPA's policies (as they do to NEPA's), but they show no evidence of following or advancing them. Litigation seeking to force compliance with section 110(d) has been limited and no more successful than litigation seeking compliance with NEPA section 101.[23] To judge from the NHPA experience, simply telling agencies to follow abstract policies doesn't work—by itself.

I suspect that agencies don't pay attention to the policy provisions of NEPA and NHPA because no one (other than the occasional plaintiff, with mostly discouraging results) insists that they do so, or tells them how to do so. The Council on Environmental Quality (CEQ) has regulations insisting on compliance with NEPA's *procedural* requirements—to prepare and circulate environmental impact statements—so the procedural requirements are followed or at least considered enough to be dodged. The Advisory Council on Historic Preservation (ACHP) has regulations governing section 106 review, and agencies usually at least go through the motions of following them—or, as with NEPA, giving them enough thought to elude them. Neither the CEQ nor the ACHP has regulations detailing how the *policies* underlying their procedures are to be attended to in the conduct of project review. It is in that context that agencies are routinely challenged to consider the environmental effects of their actions, but they're not challenged in the same context to address national NEPA and NHPA policy, so they don't. Why should they? How should they?

NEPA needs to be changed, I think—as does NHPA—but not simply by telling the agencies to attend to its policies. What's needed is a change in the action-forcing provision of NEPA—section 102—to create a structure within which agencies must address NEPA policy. Later in this chapter I'll suggest how this might be done.

Restore CEQ's Role

The question I just asked—Why should agencies address NEPA policy if they're not required to do so in the course of project review?—brings us to Caldwell's next "alternative": restoring the intended role and authority of the Council on Environmental Quality. If there were a powerful, well-directed, well-staffed CEQ with the bully pulpit provided by its place in the Executive Office of the President, it would, presumably, be able to persuade the federal establishment to do a better job by NEPA's purposes.

This is undoubtedly true. As the Army report I discussed in Chapter One emphasized,[24] agencies like the Army are far better at adhering to "bright green" environmental laws like the Clean Water Act than they are at following "light green" laws like NEPA and NHPA. This is largely because the bright green laws enjoy external enforcement. There is someone outside the action agency—usually the U.S. Environmental Protection Agency or a state equivalent—with the authority to slap wrists if the law's requirements aren't followed. Give CEQ some such authority, and it could—in theory—make the agencies shape up.

But it also might not, and it might make things worse. It's interesting that Caldwell refers to strengthening CEQ's role as a "restoration" of its authority and portrays NEPA as clearly having given the Council such authority. But the powers ascribed to CEQ by NEPA are really pretty vapid. CEQ's powers are to "appraise programs and activities" and to "be conscious of and responsive to the scientific, economic, social, esthetic, and cultural needs of the Nation." CEQ is supposed to "formulate and recommend national policies."[25] It is charged with helping the president prepare an annual report to Congress.[26] It is empowered to do studies, gather information, and advise the president.[27] Nowhere is it given the authority to lean on the agencies, to prevail on them to pay proper attention to the environment or give protective alternatives due weight in planning. Would a beefed-up, better-funded CEQ make much difference, if it were charged with nothing more than its brief as outlined in NEPA? I don't see any reason to think so.

And there are real dangers in the centralization of power. Everyone knows what power does and what absolute power does absolutely. In the CRM world, we've seen the near-absolute power that's drifted into the hands of the State Historic Preservation Officers turn some of them into the most petty of despots. And they are despots subject to political influence by their overseers, the governors and state legislators. A more powerful CEQ still lodged in the Executive Office of the President would be similarly subject to political influence. Is this the way to create an independent authority that will protect the public's interest in our heritage? The Environmental Protection Agency, which has considerable power under the Clean Air Act, Clean Water Act, and other "bright green" environmental laws, has certainly had its share of struggles with political pressure. Why would a more powerful CEQ be any different?

Of course, there's a legitimate argument that politics comprises the medium through which the will of the public is expressed. This being so, it is only appropriate and right for the overseers of government responsibility toward natural and cultural heritage to be politically directed. This would be a sensible argument if presidents were elected based even in part on clearly articulated environment/heritage policies, so the electorate really knew what they were voting for—but that's hardly the case. Such issues sway the way some of us vote, but we are always more or less buying a pig in a poke. And the fact that a candidate speaks in ringing tones in favor of abstractions like "environmental protection" and "America's heritage" doesn't telegraph very accurately how his or her administration is going to act when push comes to shove on a particular issue.

Example: We have lately engaged in a presidential contest in which environmental issues played substantial roles. Both candidates supported weaning ourselves from fossil fuels (although one subscribed to the somewhat counterintuitive idea of doing so by drilling for more) through the use of "green" technology and the development of alternative sources of power. All well and good, but even the greenest ways of powering the world have impacts. Deploying solar generators takes up land, deprives plants of sun, digs up archaeological sites, messes with people's valued viewsheds and ways of using the land. Wind farms have substantial visual impacts and kill birds. Geothermal energy production has ground-surface impacts similar to those of oil and gas extraction. An administration's support for environmentally friendly development doesn't say a thing about how wisely it will balance the interests of a "green" development project and its proponents against those of other stakeholders, other aspects of the environment. Some of the most arrogant project proponents I've encountered have draped themselves in the mantles of social responsibility. "We are *good*, so the laws don't apply to *us*."

If a beefed-up CEQ is going to help make sure that development planning is balanced, fully considers alternatives, takes into account its effects on our natural and cultural heritage, it has to be insulated to some extent from political considerations, even (perhaps particularly) when its political overseers are favorably inclined toward the environment. And it has to have a system, a process, to employ in promoting mindful adherence to NEPA's laudable principles. Merely "restoring" the role of CEQ (or its equivalent) will not do the job.

Amend the Constitution

Caldwell's last and most intriguing proposition is that we should amend the U.S. Constitution to favor environmental protection. It's probably the alternative that's least likely to happen, but in many ways it's the most easily justified.

The founding fathers, after all, did not understand the environment to be threatened, or even particularly fragile. They were products of a society in which nature was to be conquered and culture was practiced in salons. So the Constitution says nothing about the desirability of preserving natural and cultural heritage. It couldn't be expected to, any more than it could be expected to say anything about racial or gender equality.

So today, there really isn't much constitutional basis for government action to protect the environment. This is nowhere more obvious than in federal efforts to regulate dumping fill into wetlands, for which Congress had to turn to the Constitution's "commerce clause." The federal government regulates interstate commerce; waterways are critical to such commerce; wetlands feed waterways; ergo the federal government can regulate what happens to wetlands. A river of litigation has flowed from questions like how closely related a wetland has to be to a navigable waterway (how navigable? by what?) in order to be regulated. None of this has anything to do with the desirability of governmental wetland regulation.

A constitutional amendment affirming government's obligation and authority to protect the human environment would provide the basis for correcting this sort of problem. However, it would of course face stiff opposition from those who saw it (perhaps with justification) as a monstrous extension of government's long arm into their lives.

Caldwell went so far as to suggest draft language for a constitutional amendment:

> In all acts authorized or enforced by all governments of the United States, the integrity of natural systems shall not be impaired except as necessary to protect public health, safety and welfare or in response to emergencies where no socially acceptable alternative exists. Sustainability and renewal of natural systems, enhancement of environmental quality and human habitat, and fairness to present and future generations shall be governing principles of policy.[28]

I don't think this does the job at all. My bias toward the cultural aspects of heritage, of course, makes me bridle at the exclusive focus on "natural systems," but more importantly, this amendment would not solve the problem exemplified by wetlands. If we want authority to regulate dumping in wetlands, this amendment wouldn't provide it, because if government didn't already have the authority to regulate it, such dumping would not be "authorized" by the government of the United States and therefore wouldn't be subject to federal regulation—unless one interprets "all governments of the United States" to include the governments of all subdivisions of government (state governments, local governments, and so on).

On the other hand, I'd argue that Caldwell's draft goes too far, by essentially placing the integrity of natural systems superior to all other considerations of public policy except health, safety, welfare, and response to emergencies. Are things like property rights not to be considered at all?

In 2007, Representative Jesse Jackson, Jr. (D-IL) introduced a resolution in the House of Representatives calling for a constitutional amendment[29] reading as follows:

> Section 1. All persons shall have a right to a clean, safe, and sustainable environment, which right shall not be denied or abridged by the United States or any State.

> Section 2. The Congress shall have power to enforce and implement this article by appropriate legislation.

This one has the charm of simplicity and the advantages (I think) of being grounded in human rights and not elevating the environment, *qua* environment, above all other considerations. Caldwell argued that it would be difficult to interpret a rights-based amendment,[30] but Jackson's language strikes me as a good deal clearer than Caldwell's. It would require Congress and the courts to balance the right to environmental protection against other rights—like the right to the enjoyment of private property— but, to me, that makes much more sense than proposing a governmental responsibility to environmental protection that supersedes all else.

All this is pretty academic, of course; aside from Congressman Jackson's initiative, there is no current movement toward a constitutional amendment, and it's hardly to be expected in the near future.

So while they're interesting and well intentioned, I think Caldwell's prescriptions fall short of what's needed. This is at least partly the result of unexamined assumptions.

■ ■ ■ NEVER *&^%$#@ ASSUME!

When the younger of my sons was an impressionable preteen, he was much taken by the writings of Richard Marcinko, a former U.S. Navy SEAL. Marcinko's first book[31] was a semi-autobiographical novel about his adventures in Viet Nam and as a SEAL trainer; among the rules he emphasized to his trainees was: "Never #$%^&^*& assume!" Never assume there isn't a bad guy with an AK-47 in the closet, or that your buddy has your back.

Marcinko's motto comes to mind whenever I read complaints like Caldwell's, and those of Lindstrom and Smith, that the agencies and the courts have misinterpreted NEPA by failing to insist on adherence to section 101's policies. It seems to me that these writers, like NEPA's authors, assume a great deal. And it's turned out that the bad guy with the Kalashnikov has been there.

Consider NEPA's core procedural requirement: that agencies

> include in every recommendation or report on proposals for legislation and other major Federal actions significantly affecting the quality of the human environment, a detailed

statement by the responsible official on (i) the environmental impact of the proposed action, (ii) any adverse environmental effects which cannot be avoided should the proposal be implemented, (iii) alternatives to the proposed action, (iv) the relationship between local short-term uses of man's environment and the maintenance and enhancement of long-term productivity, and (v) any irreversible and irretrievable commitments of resources which would be involved in the proposed action should it be implemented.[32]

What did the authors of this language assume? What did they leave unsaid that they should have said?

First, there are those famous words: "significantly affecting the quality of the human environment." What constitutes a "significant" effect, or "quality," or for that matter the "human environment?" These terms were left for CEQ to define in regulation, and CEQ did a pretty good job. At least they defined "human environment" rather elegantly[33] and thoughtfully crafted a set of variables to consider in determining "significance."[34] But the statute is also silent on how an agency is to decide whether a given action may *have* significant effects, and the regulations did a fairly miserable job of clarifying that. Agencies are directed to prepare environmental assessments (EAs) but are given almost no direction about how to do it, or how to use the EA in determining the significance of impacts.[35] NEPA's authors, and more crucially the authors of the CEQ regulations, simply assumed that agencies would figure out how to make this critical determination. They went on to wax eloquent (well, at least wordy) about how to write and process environmental impact statements (EISs). As it has turned out, it is in the process of EA preparation that some of the greatest abuses take place. The EA is a Kalashnikov in the closet.

More fundamentally, the authors of NEPA seem to have held at least two naïve assumptions about the "detailed statement" that agencies were called upon to make. One was that the statement—the EIS—would be an honest one. Based on this assumption, the statute never says that EISs have to be honest or unbiased. Again, CEQ tried to correct this problem with regulatory language—notably the "integrity" language we touched on earlier[36]—but it's easy for agencies and consultants to say, "Oh yeah, we have integrity," without giving much thought to the matter. I imagine—because I've encountered the attitude in my own regulation-writing career—that no one wanted to be so gauche as to suggest that a federal agency would be anything but honest and unbiased in its appraisal of environmental impacts. Another Kalashnikov.

Another naïve assumption was that the "statement" would play a meaningful role in agency decision making. Here, I think, is where the section 101 policy statements truly fell through the cracks. The law says "make a statement," but what is one supposed to do with the statement? It is to be made public and shared with the president and CEQ, and it is to "accompany the proposal through the existing agency review processes."[37] We are not told how the agency is to use it, what role it should play in agency planning. Here is where the law, and/or the regulations, could have insisted that decisions actually be informed by the statements of impact and be justified in terms of the section 101 policies, but neither did so. The regulations do state, in their introductory paragraph, that

> [t]he President, the federal agencies, and the courts share responsibility for enforcing the Act so as to achieve the substantive requirements of section 101.[38]

But that is *all* they say. It's assumed that the agencies, together with the president and the courts, would carry out this responsibility without being instructed in how to do it. Partly as a result, NEPA has come to be understood as requiring the preparation of documents, but not requiring that such documents be used for anything.

What's remarkable to me is that much of the angst that NEPA's academic critics experience seems to arise from the same assumptions that plagued NEPA's authors—and from disbelief that anyone could fail to share them. Why haven't the courts insisted that agencies follow section 101's policies? Well, courts can do strange things, but it hasn't helped that the law doesn't say the policies have to be followed. More importantly, it doesn't spell out how the policies are to be *used*. Why have the agencies so often treated NEPA as a bothersome technicality? Lots of reasons, no doubt, but it hasn't helped that neither the law nor the regulations tell them to treat it otherwise.

I don't mean to be insulting in challenging Caldwell's assumptions and those of NEPA's other authors and interpreters. But I simply don't think it would help to rewrite NEPA or enact a constitutional amendment without carefully considering our assumptions and without understanding how our creations are likely to be interpreted and played out on the ground. I hope the preceding chapters have gone some way toward advancing that understanding.

■ ■ ■ SIMPLIFYING THE SOLUTION

If Caldwell's prescriptions won't work without the very change in public understanding he prescribes, then is there anything to be done to make EIA and CRM work the way their creators envisioned? Or maybe even better? I think so.

At the core of the suite of problems we've discussed are three serious deficiencies with the statutes themselves and with the regulations they generated.

1   Neither the statutes nor the regulations give agencies clear direction to apply the national policies they prescribe, in the course of doing the nitty-gritty procedural things the regulations *do* direct agencies to do.

2   Neither the statutes nor the regulations take human nature into account; they assume a level of integrity and a clarity of vision that it is entirely unrealistic to expect of agency officials, project proponents, and for-profit consultants.

3   The procedures for involving the public laid out in the NEPA regulations are worthless. Those prescribed by the section 106 regulations are better in concept, but too twisted and narrowly applied in practice. The result is that we cannot even begin to build the public support needed to make any of Caldwell's dreams come true.

We are not going to correct these deficiencies—to say nothing of promoting a sense of heritage stewardship in the American people and their representatives in Congress—in one fell swoop, one stroke of some executive pen. But there is a start that could be made, some small actions that would make a difference, and that would lay the groundwork for more substantial fixes farther down the road. Some of these actions *could* be done at the stroke of a pen, provided the penmanship were exercised at 1600 Pennsylvania Avenue.

■ ■ ■ MEMO TO PRESIDENT OBAMA

So with consummate hubris, I'll bring this book to a close with recommendations to the president who'll take office about the time it is published. Mister President, if you think it's worthwhile to stop wasting everybody's time and money whitewashing the impacts of federal actions and decisions on our natural and cultural heritage, here are a few things to do.

Tell the Agencies to Clean Up Their Acts

Issue an executive order telling all agencies of the federal government to establish or rework their procedures for compliance with the heritage laws—notably but not exclusively NEPA and NHPA—to ensure, to the extent possible, that the studies that are done and the reports that are prepared are free from bias in favor of or against the actions whose impacts are analyzed. Go on to direct that such procedures provide for things such as:

1   Conducting impact analyses—of all kinds, not just EISs—using knowledgeable third parties with no direct or indirect links to the proponent of the actions whose impacts are analyzed.

2   Conducting rigorous third-party review and critique of any analyses performed by or on behalf of project proponents.

3   Objectively analyzing alternatives, including those suggested by members of the public.

4 Consulting with affected and interested parties and the general public to identify and resolve objections and explore alternatives, with the objective of reaching agreements among all concerned parties (with provision for a final decision to be made in the absence of agreement). It should be made very clear that while expert opinion is important, so are the opinions of ordinary citizens, especially where places and things that citizens value are concerned.

5 Considering *all* kinds of project effects—direct effects, indirect effects, and crucially, how the alternatives under review would contribute to cumulative effects.

6 Considering not only quantifiable impacts but those that can't be quantified, such as effects on social, cultural, and spiritual values.

7 Integrating and coordinating analysis and consultation under all the environmental and heritage laws, regulations, and executive orders, notably including NEPA, NHPA, and ESA.

8 Regular training for agency and contractor personnel, cooperation with academic institutions, and other such measures designed to maintain the quality of interdisciplinary research and responsible consultation with the public.

9 Monitoring performance to promote integrity in analysis and in relations with the public.

10 Actually *using* the results of impact analysis in making decisions, with explicit attention to the policies set forth in section 101 of NEPA and section 2 of NHPA. An agency should be able to show either that a decision it makes is consistent with these policies or that its inconsistency is justified in the public interest.

I know, Mister President, that a lot of these things seem so obvious that you shouldn't need tFo instruct your establishment in them, but believe me, you do. And doing so would be a start at reforming the system, both by improving its integrity and by getting the public actively involved.

There's something else you should do.

Rework the Regulations and Consider Consolidation

Tell CEQ, the Advisory Council on Historic Preservation, the Fish and Wildlife Service, and all the other oversight agencies to get together over a specified period of time, with lots of public participation, to reconsider and revise their collective regulations implementing NEPA, NHPA, and the other heritage laws. The agencies should seek consistency, simplicity, transparency, and full, open consultation with the public.

Direct the same agencies, perhaps through the same program of cooperative review, to come up with recommendations for consolidating compliance with the various laws, including changes in the laws themselves, as needed, to create an EIA system (including CRM) that is simple, straightforward, and accessible to the public.

Make sure the cooperative interagency review is overseen and coordinated by someone with the authority to resolve disputes and gore whoever's oxen need goring.[39] Consolidation of oversight agency functions is certainly going to leave blood on the floor, but it has to be done if a system is to be created that ordinary citizens, not just specialists, can understand and participate in.

And then . . .

Consider Legislation

Once you have an idea of what ought to be done to improve the review systems, and once you've explored how far you can go under existing authorities, go to Congress with a package of legislative adjustments to NEPA, NHPA, and the other laws. Some might simply be done away with. For instance, there would be no need for a section 106 of NHPA if NEPA provided for public consultation about impacts on the cultural aspects of the environment. Others could be adjusted. For instance, rather than just calling for a "statement" of environmental impacts, NEPA might prescribe a process of analysis, consultation, and application of the section 101 policies.

Whatever law or laws emerged from this process should clearly embody the principles of honest, balanced analysis and consultative public participation. The law should not elevate heritage protection over everything else, but it should make sure that such protection, and the interests of people who care about their heritage, have a fair chance to influence public policy.

As for the Constitution

None of the above actions will thicken up the painfully thin attention given natural and cultural heritage—and other aspects of the environment—by the Constitution. That needs to be fixed too. Congressman Jackson's bill seems like a good start. But there's no need to wait for a constitutional amendment—or even legislation—to begin adjusting our EIA and CRM systems so they do what their creators intended, rather than merely wasting time and money and generating frustration.

■ ■ ■ A LAST WORD ABOUT OBJECTIVITY

Throughout this book I've bewailed the lack of objectivity in the studies conducted under the heritage laws. But is objectivity something to which we can realistically aspire?

The Australian scholar Sharon Beder thinks not.

> Environmental Impact Statements (EISs) have lost credibility with environmental and resident groups over recent years because they are being increasingly perceived as biased public relations documents. This arises in part because the community generally expects that an EIS should be an objective scientific report whilst many consultants and project proponents view an EIS as a supporting document prepared as part of the procedure for gaining approval for a project.

> The goal of a completely objective document is illusory because science itself is socially constructed. This is exacerbated by the circumstances of EIS preparation where large investments, careers and the viability of businesses are at stake. It is therefore inevitable that the values and goals of those preparing an EIS will shape its contents and conclusions through the way scientific data is collected, analysed, interpreted and presented.[40]

Beder's argument reflects a postmodern perspective in which objectivity is seen as unrealistic in virtually any human enterprise—even the physical sciences. I think the argument is correct, and what's true for physics applies in spades to the softer sciences, social sciences, and humanistic disciplines that contribute to EIA and CRM. Perhaps we can objectively measure the parts per million of gunk in the water or air, but the ways we interpret these measurements in terms of human or environmental health always reflect degrees of subjectivity. Issues like the carrying capacity of an ecosystem or the potential effects of a temperature change are more subjective yet. When we come to subjects like the social and cultural values that people ascribe to aspects of their natural and cultural heritage, objectivity simply doesn't compute.

But fairness does. Balance does. Being open-minded does. These, surely, we can aspire to. Analyses in EIA and CRM should be fair; they should be balanced; they should be open to the interests and concerns of all. If they're not, then why do them?

And even if we can never realistically claim to be unbiased or objective, that doesn't mean that the concept is meaningless. It's not a violation of law or logic for a quantum physicist to act in daily life as though Newtonian physics ruled the universe, even though physicists know it does not. Similarly, it seems to me that to have integrity in our practice of EIA and CRM, we have to act as though objective analysis and unbiased decision making were achievable, and seek to achieve them, even though we know it's probably impossible to do so.

So, how can we promote more objective, unbiased analyses in EIA and CRM? I think we need to acknowledge that it is unrealistic to expect people or agencies to do them just because they're told to. If Congress were to pass a law directing me to perform an unbiased analysis of my grandchildren's intellectual abilities relative to those of someone else's, I might make an honest effort, but it's very unlikely I'd succeed. In the same way, it's hardly realistic to expect the Corps of Engineers or the Bureau of Land Management to be objective in analyzing the impacts of projects they (or others to whose interests they are obliged to be sensitive) want to do. This is particularly the case when Congress itself sends mixed messages—on the one hand seeking honest analyses of environmental impacts, and on the other directing agencies to "streamline review"—expedite moving projects through those silly environmental "clearances."

We need to build administrative systems that, as much as possible, separate impact analysis from the interests of project proponents, and make those systems as open as possible to public participation and critique. There are probably ways to do this other than those I've outlined in this chapter—just as there are problems with EIA and CRM that I've not touched on in this book and horror stories I've not recounted. But I hope at least that this book can stimulate some discussion of possibilities.

■ ■ ■ As the Seas Rise

I've often paused in writing this book, sometimes for hours, sometimes for months, overcome by the feeling that I'm fiddling while Rome burns. What earthly point is there, I ask myself, in diddling about with adjustments in the way we consider environmental impacts—and impacts on things like old buildings and archaeological sites, for heaven's sake— when the atmosphere's warming, the polar ice is melting, the seas are rising? Doing fieldwork as I sometimes do on a Pacific atoll, I can see the water rising, and I doubt if anything is going to save a host of island nations and a lot of continental waterfront from inundation. The costs of this disaster in terms of natural and cultural heritage—including living, functioning human populations and their social systems—will be far beyond anything we can imagine measuring or mitigating.

But be this as it may, it seems to me that the American people deserve to have effective ways to influence what government does to their—our—

heritage. And I cheer myself—faintly, dimly, half-heartedly—with the belief that EIA and CRM may, if they're improved, make some small contributions to ameliorating the effects of global climate change. All those displaced islanders and coastal residents will have to be housed and fed; all those coastal cities and industries, farms and forests will have to be relocated or replaced. The impacts of all these adjustments may be greater in some ways than the impacts of climate change itself. And unlike climate change, these impacts will be subject to human control, human influence. EIA and CRM can help governments manage these impacts so that we don't inadvertently do more damage than necessary to achieve the adaptations we will have to make. But if all we have to work with is the EIA/CRM industry as it is presently constituted, we will only be wasting money that could be better spent building floating cities or seeking another planet to despoil.

AFTERWORD Property Rights, Money, and Inertia

Late in November 2008, I posted a *précis* of this book on my blog (*http://crmplus.blogspot.com/*). Among those who responded before my deadline for completing the manuscript was Ira Beckerman of the Pennsylvania Department of Transportation. Ira allowed me to summarize and respond to his comments—which, I should probably stress, don't reflect any kind of official PennDOT position. Ira's comments, posted complete on my blog, refer mostly to the National Historic Preservation Act (NHPA). He says:

> In thousands of pages of legislation, regulation, guidance, and policy is there anything that directs (agencies) to protect anything? The short answer is no. So the fair question is "what are we doing with all that time, money, and effort if not protecting resources?"
>
> This is the point at which I am . . . diverging from Tom King. He sees the problem as due to the frailties in people and institutions, which are resistant to repair because of bureaucratic inertia or fear of massive negative changes once the laws are in play. It has been my experience that even if (these) weren't problems, . . . the outcomes would be the same.
>
> Both NEPA and NHPA are "process" laws. They do not specify an outcome . . . but a process (to) be followed that in principle leads to preservation. What I have found is a good process does not necessarily yield a good result.
>
> One of the deeper reasons we don't preserve much has . . . to do with how Americans conceive of private property in

relation to the common "weal." Getting the public and the electorate to buy into the notion that some resources transcend private property is a very tough sell indeed.

Working hand in hand with private property views is the very American notion that history is bunk. Hence the lack of public support for strong historic preservation legislation or enforcement. It's not the bad guys in Washington. It's all of us telling the guys in Washington we value development and progress over the past.

I sympathize with Ira, but I'm a fan of good process, and I don't believe that preservation is always the "good" outcome of NHPA section 106 review. Section 106 review should seek the public interest, which is sometimes in preservation, sometimes quite elsewhere. And even if one despises the sanctity of private property rights (I don't), I don't think it's practical to pin one's hopes on a sea change in our national political philosophy. Or on better history (or environmental) education, for that matter, though there's no question that such education is badly needed.

As it turns out, Ira doesn't really hitch his wagon entirely to the stars of philosophical transformation and educational reform. He goes on to "assume for the moment that we aren't going to go into the private property zone and aren't going to start a major history education initiative," and offers the following recommendations to the Obama administration:

1   We need Supreme Court Justices that can balance private property rights with the common weal. It's been too one-sided for too long.

2   Revisit the linkage between the National Register and Section 106. What is needed in 106 is a way to objectively value properties without dragging the formal process of the National Register into it.

3   Transparency is good, but the public needs to be able to read the process. As part of any agency's participation in NEPA or NHPA should be an ongoing and active education effort for the public to make them capable of working as full partners in preservation.

4   Push mitigation banking. Like a cap and trade greenhouse gas program, create a currency in preservation and impacts and allow agen-

cies to buy their way out of problems. Set up the program so that the funds can be used for active preservation, including property acquisition. Don't make it too cheap.

5   Create a national licensing for historic preservation specialists, along the lines of licensing for other professionals, including doctors, lawyers, and professional engineers.

To which I'll respond briefly as follows:

1   Sure. Here's hoping.

2   As I've implied in Chapter Eight and argued elsewhere, we could easily do without the National Register in the section 106 process, and indeed without section 106, if NEPA were reformed by grafting onto it the consultation requirements now found only in section 106 review.

3   I don't think we can realistically expect the public to get educated about section 106 and NEPA until we make the review procedures a lot more (a) relevant to what real people, as well as specialists, care about, and (b) straightforward and sensible. Educating citizens to deal with the sort of esoterica we "experts" spout and manipulate is a losing game, as it should be.

4–5 Cap and trade is intriguing, and licensing may be a good idea, though my experience with licensing archaeologists has made me deeply suspicious of it, and it's certainly no panacea.

Richard Galloway, a graduate anthropology student at the University of Alaska, also responded, and we've engaged in a lively correspondence, ongoing as this is written. With his permission, I'll try to summarize.

In a nutshell, Richard raises two issues. First, he asks where the money's going to come from:

> Most of the changes you suggest are good solid changes, but the fact remains that to implement any of those changes will require more manpower or more funds or both, and given the economic climate currently I don't think there is going to be

any increase in tax dollars to the government agencies to do the work or contract out the work to meet the ideals of the CRM and EIA processes.

Acknowledging that I may be a cockeyed optimist, I responded that I didn't—don't—think the changes I propose should cost money; instead they ought to save it. I wrote:

> Most of the humongous costs I see incurred in the course of EIA and CRM are incurred for stupid reasons and devoted to dumb things; they're costs that could be prevented by doing a better job up front.

In response to which, Richard raised his second point: that inertia is hard to fight.

> I agree fully on this, but it goes back to the issue of "change" and how resistant people are to changing the status quo. If we can get the process started earlier in the game, it would not cost as much. The question is, how do we get the CRM [sic: and EIA] people involved in the planning stages, not in the later, building process? . . . To make this happen you would have to have teams of people, or a very well trained individual, brought into the planning process from the very start of a project. . . . The people in power don't see a need to comply with the laws early; it does not cost them enough dollars to get their attention. The workers directly involved are seldom the ones who make the final decisions, and those making the decisions are only looking at costs.

Our conversation has gone in several directions from this point, and it continues, but I'll claim author's privilege here and wind up with my thoughts on institutional change. I acknowledged to Richard again that I may be overly optimistic, but my experience suggests that such change can be forced. I wrote:

> For instance: Back in 1972, Richard Nixon issued Executive Order 11593, in essence directing federal agencies to treat places that were eligible for the National Register as though they were already on it—section 106, in those days, applying

only to registered properties. Nothing much would probably have happened in response to the EO, except that NPS assigned three guys—*three guys!*— as "executive order consultants," whose job it was to go around to the agencies and lobby them to get into compliance, and help them figure out how. For all practical purposes (and for better or worse), these guys created CRM in this country. Within maybe five years, every major agency had some kind of program up and running, and the CRM contracting business had taken off. We can debate whether these were good things, . . . but the fact remains that change happened in the ways agencies dealt with historic properties, and it happened because of (a) high level policy direction and (b) programmed action by one of the major oversight agencies.

Money is an issue, but strange things can happen with money in hard times. I'm reminded that federal spending on such things as conservation, historic preservation, and archaeology had its birth, for all practical purposes, in the New Deal—that is, in governmental responses to the Great Depression. And I do think that a reformed, reimagined EIA/CRM system could not only do a better job of protecting our heritage but do it more efficiently, at less cost. As for overcoming inertia, it all boils down to leadership. We haven't had any in the EIA and CRM games for the last decade or more, but maybe we can get some as a tiny part of the change that so many of us recently were inspired to support in the voting booth.

All Those Bloody Acronyms

*A*cronymous speech and writing—using lots of acronyms in place of long titles—is one tool that agencies, consultants, and project proponents use to befuddle the public. But acronyms are also unavoidable—or at least, I've not figured out a way to avoid them—when writing about laws, programs, and other entities with multi-word titles. So I've used acronyms pretty liberally throughout this book, trying to define them repeatedly enough to minimize confusion. So in each chapter, the first time I use an acronym I put it in parentheses following the full term it refers to—"Council on Environmental Quality (CEQ)." Even within a chapter, if I haven't used an acronym in a few pages, when I use it again I generally define it again. But for ease of reference, here's an overall acronym glossary:

ACHP—Advisory Council on Historic Preservation

AIRFA—American Indian Religious Freedom Act

APE—Area of potential effect

BLM—Bureau of Land Management

BNSF—Burlington Northern Santa Fe Railroad

BPS—Buckland Preservation Society

BTR—Between the (Cumberland and Tennessee) Rivers

CAA—Clean Air Act

CATEX (or CX, CatEx, etc.)—Categorical exclusion under NEPA

CEQ—Council on Environmental Quality

CERCLA—Comprehensive Environmental Response, Compensation and Liability Act

CERCLIS—Comprehensive Environmental Response, Compensation and Liability Information System

CRM—Cultural resource management

CWA—Clean Water Act

DEIS—Draft environmental impact statement

EA—Environmental assessment

EIA—Environmental impact assessment

EIS—Environmental impact statement

EJ—Environmental justice

EPA—Environmental Protection Agency

ESA—Endangered Species Act

FEIS—Final environmental impact statement

FERC—Federal Energy Regulatory Commission

FEMA—Federal Emergency Management Agency

FHWA—Federal Highway Administration

FONSI (also called FNSI)—Finding of no significant impact

FWS—Fish and Wildlife Service

GSA—General Services Administration

HRH—Her Royal Highness

IEDR—Institute for Environmental Dispute Resolution

MOA—Memorandum of agreement (under NHPA section 106)

NAAQS—National Ambient Air Quality Standards

NAEP—National Association of Environmental Professionals

NASA—National Aeronautics and Space Administration

NEPA—National Environmental Policy Act

NHPA—National Historic Preservation Act

NMF—National Marine Fisheries Service

NOI—Notice of intent (to prepare an EIS)

NPS—National Park Service

NRHP—National Register of Historic Places

NTHP—National Trust for Historic Preservation

PG&E—Pacific Gas and Electric Company

PEIS—Programmatic environmental impact statement[1]

RCRA—Resource Conservation and Recovery Act

RFRA—Religious Freedom Restoration Act

ROD—Record of decision under NEPA

SEIS—Supplemental environmental impact statement

SHPO—State Historic Preservation Officer

TCP—Traditional cultural property (or place)

THPO—Tribal Historic Preservation Officer

TVA—Tennessee Valley Authority

Chapter One

1 *http://whc.unesco.org/en/about/*.

2 David Rubenson, Jerry Aroesty, and Charles Thompsen, *Two Shades of Green: Environmental Protection and Combat Training* (Rand Arroyo Center, 1992); see *http://www.rand.org/pubs/reports/2007/R4220.pdf*, accessed September 2, 2008.

3 The Army study calls them, a bit inaccurately, "rule-based."

4 Or "planning" laws, in the vernacular of the Army study.

5 There are others—at the federal, state, and local level—but they all work (if they work) more or less the same way the laws I'll discuss do.

6 Virtually every other country has developed similar laws, or law-like requirements, as have the various international development agencies. Examining the international EIA and CRM games is well beyond the scope of anything I could undertake, so this book focuses on the United States.

7 Lynton Keith Caldwell, *The National Environmental Policy Act: An Agenda for the Future* (Bloomington: Indiana University Press, 1998).

8 Matthew J. Lindstrom and Zachary A. Smith, *The National Environmental Policy Act: Judicial Misconstruction, Legislative Indifference, and Executive Neglect* (College Station: Texas A&M University Press, 2001).

9 Frank Fischer, *Citizens, Experts, and the Environment: The Politics of Local Knowledge* (Durham, NC: Duke University Press, 2000).

10 40 CFR 1500–1508—that is, parts 1500 through 1508 of title 40 of the Code of Federal Regulations; see *http://ceq.hss.doe.gov/Nepa/regs/ceq/toc_ceq.htm*.

11 36 CFR 800—in other words, part 800 of title 36 of the Code of Federal Regulations; see *www.achp.gov*.

12 See *http://www.fws.gov/endangered/*, accessed August 28, 2008.

13 See *http://www.usace.army.mil/cw/cecwo/reg/sadmin3.htm*, accessed August 28, 2008.

14 See *http://www.fema.gov/plan/ehp/ehplaws/eo11988.shtm*, accessed August 28, 2008.

15 See (for instance) *http://www.welcomehome.org/rainbow/nfs-regs/rfra-act.html* and *http://www.nps.gov/history/local-law/FHPL_IndianRelFreAct.pdf*, accessed August 28, 2008.

16 See *http://www.epa.gov/Compliance/environmentaljustice/*, accessed August 28, 2008.

17 Leslie Wildesen of Environmental Training and Consulting International (ETCI) has elegantly summarized much of what has gone wrong with NEPA during the Bush

administration in a white paper for the Obama transition team, serialized on ETCI's web site: *http://web.me.com/envirotrain/TEB/The_Environmental_Blog/The_Environmental_Blog.html*.

[18] *Comanche Nation, et al. v. United States of America, et al.*, 5:08-cv-0849-D, U.S. District Court for the Western District of Oklahoma, September 23, 2008.

[19] See *http://ceq.hss.doe.gov/ntf/*, accessed August 28, 2008.

[20] See *www.achp.gov*, accessed August 28, 2008.

[21] The Rosas have given up their fight and settled with the railroad, which has resulted in taking down their excellent web site on the project. The local Sierra Club chapter web site provides an overview that I think is pretty accurate; see *http://riogrande. sierraclub.org/campaigns/abo_canyon/abo_canyon.htm*, accessed August 28, 2008.

[22] See *http://www.bucklandva.org/*, accessed August 28, 2008.

[23] See *http://www.californiachronicle.com/articles/16414*, accessed August 28, 2008.

[24] In CRM jargon, the Maze landscape is what's known as a "traditional cultural property." For details on such properties, see T. F. King, *Places That Count: Traditional Cultural Properties in Cultural Resource Management* (Walnut Creek, CA: AltaMira Press, 2003).

[25] See *http://www.betweentherivers.org/*, accessed August 28, 2008.

[26] See *http://leftofdayton.wordpress.com/2008/03/16/how-piketon-ohio-became-a-potemkin-villageby-geoffrey-sea/*, accessed August 28, 2008.

[27] See, for instance, *http://www.granitehillsdesign.com/cds/issues.html*, accessed August 28, 2008.

[28] They've apparently lost; see *http://www.ferc.gov/legal/court-cases/opinions/2008/05-1421.pdf*, accessed August 28, 2008.

[29] See *http://www.savejeanklockpark.org/*, accessed August 28, 2008.

[30] My report to the commission is at *http://klamathsalmonlibrary.org/documents/King2004pd.pdf*, accessed August 28, 2008.

[31] See, for instance, *http://www.sacredland.org/endangered_sites_pages/mt_graham.html* on Mt. Graham, and *http://www.sacredland.org/endangered_sites_pages/mauna_kea.html* on Mauna Kea. I can find no web site that gives the tribe's side of the Kitt Peak story, but *http://www.noao.edu/outreach/kptour/kpno_tohono.html* gives the observatory's perspective.

[32] See R. Bass, A. Herson, and K. Bogdan, *The NEPA Book* (Point Arena, CA: Solano Press, 2001); Larry W. Canter, *Environmental Impact Assessment* (New York: McGraw-Hill, 1995); Council on Environmental Quality, *A Citizen's Guide to the NEPA* (Washington, DC: 2007); Charles H. Eccleston, *Environmental Impact Statements: A Comprehensive Guide to Project and Strategic Planning* (New York: Wiley, 2000), and *NEPA and Environmental Planning: Tools, Techniques, and Approaches for Practitioners* (Boca Raton, FL: CRC Press, 2008); Environmental Law Institute, *Rediscovering the National Environmental Policy Act: Back to the Future* (New York: 1995); Valerie Fogleman, *Guide to the National Environmental Policy Act: Interpretations, Applications, and Compliance* (New York: Quorum, 1990); Stephen G. Hildebrand, *Environmental Analysis: The NEPA Experience* (Boca Raton, FL: CRC Press, 1993); Bram F. Noble, *Introduction to Environmental Impact Assessment: A Guide to Principles and Practice* (New York: Oxford University Press, 2005).

[33] See Advisory Council on Historic Preservation, *Protecting Historic Properties: A Citizen's Guide to Section 106 Review* (Washington, DC: 2002); T. F. King, *Saving Places That Matter: A Citizen's Guide to the National Historic Preservation Act* (Walnut Creek, CA: Left Coast Press, 2007); *Cultural Resource Laws and Practice*, 3rd ed. (Lanham, MD: AltaMira Press, 2008). Several other books have "cultural resource management" in their titles but are mostly or entirely about archaeology.

Chapter Two

[1] See *http://www.naep.org//AM/Template.cfm?Section=Home*, accessed September 15, 2008.

[2] The United States is by no means alone in its laissez-faire approach to EIA and CRM; abuses in Canada, Australia, and the United Kingdom have drawn considerable fire in recent years. For a recent, typical example, see Obaidullah Nadeem and Riizwan Hameed, Evaluation of Environmental Impact Assessment System in Pakistan, *Environmental Impact Assessment Review* 28/8:562–571, Elsevier, Amsterdam.

[3] *http://cardin.senate.gov/issues/record.cfm?id=296953&*, accessed September 15, 2008.

[4] *http://www.commondreams.org/news2007/1130-02.htm*, accessed September 15, 2008.

[5] *http://findarticles.com/p/articles/mi_hb6412/is_200002/ai_n26565784*, accessed September 15, 2008.

[6] *http://www.state.nv.us/nucwaste/news2008/pdf/nv080408wyka.pdf*, accessed September 15, 2008.

[7] *http://www.ombwatch.org/article/articleview/3166/1/219?TopicID=1*, accessed September 15, 2008.

[8] *http://www.bigcitiesbigboxes.com/*, accessed September 15, 2008.

[9] *http://www.hawaiireporter.com/story.aspx?title=Navy's+Narrowly+Focused+Scoping+Meetings+Ignore+Assessing+Future+and+Past+Environmental+Risks*, accessed September 15, 2008.

[10] See these three related documents: *Abó Canyon Cultural Resource Survey, Valencia and Socorro Counties, New Mexico*, Teresa Hurt, Principal Investigator (Albuquerque: HDR Engineering Inc., July 2005); an "addendum" with the same title, same date, same Principal Investigator; and *A Plan for Archaeological Testing at Thirteen Sites Located along the Proposed New BNSF Railroad Alignment in Abó Canyon, Socorro and Valencia Counties, New Mexico*, Teresa Hurt, Principal Investigator (Albuquerque: HDR Engineering Inc., July 2005).

[11] The section 106 regulations require considering impacts on places within a broadly defined "area of potential effects," which is supposed to be established based on all kinds of possible project impacts, not just direct physical destruction. And they unequivocally define destruction of a historic property as an adverse effect on it.

[12] 40 CFR 1508.7.

[13] 40 CFR 1502.24.

Chapter Three

[1] BLM EA, App. J, p. 11.

[2] *Albuquerque Journal* article included in BLM EA, App. J.

3 Letter of March 27, 2007, Donald Borda of Corps of Engineers to Richard Alvidrez, attorney for the Rosas.

4 NEPA, at section 102(C), requires that an agency prepare a "detailed statement of environmental impacts" on any "major federal action significantly affecting the quality of the human environment." The NEPA regulations say that any action with significant effects is automatically "major," so the key issue to be determined is whether the impacts are likely to be significant.

5 Memorandum dated April 11, 2006, by James Wood, Corps of Engineers Project Manager, entitled "Meeting during Permit Evaluation, Action No. 2005 00269," Albuquerque District Corps of Engineers.

6 BLM does do "programmatic environmental assessments" on major leasing programs in given regions, but these are so general that they can't articulate potential impacts with any precision, or prescribe much to protect the environment besides compliance with NEPA and section 106—a pretty circular excuse for impact assessment.

7 See *http://www.law.cornell.edu/uscode/16/usc_sup_01_16_10_30.html*, accessed August 28, 2008.

8 Dugongs off Okinawa; see *http://www.earthjustice.org/library/legal_docs/dugong-decision-12408.pdf*, accessed August 28, 2008; for discussion see *http://journals.cambridge.org/action/displayAbstract;jsessionid=A74700720E217B7C58C30861EDB22690.tomcat1?fromPage=online&aid=545356*, accessed August 28, 2008.

Chapter Four

1 From *Environmental Assessment of the Kodiak Launch Complex, Kodiak Island, Alaska*, by Brown and Root Environmental for the Alaska Aerospace Development Corporation and the Federal Aviation Administration, May 1996, *http://www.mda.mil/mdalink/pdf/kodiakea5_96.pdf*, accessed July 6, 2008.

2 Draft "Memorandum of Agreement among Federal Highway Administration; U.S. Army Garrison; Fort Belvoir; Department of the Army, U.S. Army Corps of Engineers, Humphreys Engineer Center, Virginia State Historic Preservation Officer; Virginia Department of Transportation; Advisory Council on Historic Preservation; National Trust for Historic Preservation; Catawba Indian Nation, and Fairfax County, Virginia, with Concurrence in this MOA by Other Consulting Parties, Regarding Construction of Richmond Highway-Telegraph Road Connector (also known as Mulligan Road) in Fairfax County, Virginia," Federal Highway Administration, May, 2008.

3 *http://www.shipleygroup.com/news/0611.html* (accessed July 8, 2008). And I imagine he knows that the plural of "minimum" isn't "minimums," but he figures that you don't, and he's trying to communicate.

4 Including "the Needles," after which the California town is named and where Snoopy's cousin Spike resides.

5 For an image, see *http://www.satellite-sightseer.com/id/4179* (accessed August 9, 2008).

6 Or maybe not. As this is written, there's increasing evidence that the plume is going away naturally, albeit slowly, and may just have to be monitored while nature takes its course (unless the engineers feel they need to be seen actually *doing something* out there; but that's another issue altogether).

7 PG&E insists that it's not required to do NEPA analysis, probably because of some odd language in the Superfund law that appears to exempt remediation projects from such

review. The project is being reviewed at the state level under the NEPA-like California Environmental Quality Act.

8   Letter of April 14, 2008, BLM Arizona State Director Elaine Y. Zielinski to Fort Mojave Indian Tribal Chairman Timothy Williams.

9   It's a common principle in government that no one ever signs what they write, or writes what they sign.

Chapter Five

1   36 CFR 800.2(c)(1).

2   40 CFR 1500-1508.

3   40 CFR 1504.

4   See *http://www.epa.gov/compliance/resources/policies/ej/index.html*, accessed September 15, 2008.

5   See *http://www.epa.gov/compliance/nepa/eisdata.html*, accessed September 15, 2008.

6   See *http://www.epa.gov/superfund/sites/npl/hrsres/fact/sascreen.pdf*, accessed September 15, 2008.

7   See *http://www.ecr.gov/Default.aspx* , accessed September 15, 2008.

8   The ACHP's *Citizen's Guide to Section 106* (*http://www.achp.gov/citizensguide.html*, accessed September 15, 2008) is a good overview of the process and how a citizen can, in theory, use it.

9   National Register web site, *http://www.nationalregisterofhistoricplaces.com/*.

10   See T. F. King, *Places That Count: Traditional Cultural Properties in Cultural Resource Management* (Walnut Creek, CA: AltaMira Press, 2003), pp. 223–224, for further discussion of the Cushman project.

11   Besides in the fifty states, SHPOs operate in the District of Columbia, Puerto Rico, the Virgin Islands, Guam, American Samoa, the Commonwealth of the Northern Mariana Islands, the Republic of Palau, the Federated States of Micronesia, and the Republic of the Marshall Islands participate in the U.S. national historic preservation program.

12   36 CFR 800.2(c)(1)(i).

13   The term is one that Patricia Parker and I made up when writing a "bulletin" publication for the National Register in the late 1980s. See *http://www.nps.gov/history/nR/publications/bulletins/nrb38/*, accessed July 8, 2008.

14   To say nothing of its significance in nineteenth- and twentieth-century ranching, which continues today.

15   See *http://www.preserveala.org/_OLDDOCUMENTS/PDF/revisedsurveyguidelines.pdf*, accessed July 8, 2008.

Chapter Six

1   In the Gettysburg Address; see *http://www.yale.edu/lawweb/avalon/gettyb.htm*, accessed September 15, 2008.

2   In Isaiah 1:18; see *http://www.biblegateway.com/passage/?search=Isaiah+1:18*, accessed September 15, 2008.

3   36 CFR 800.16(f).

4 http://www.johncleesetraining.com/Decisions_Decisions_John_Cleese.htm, accessed August 10, 2008

5 Roger Fisher and William Ury, *Getting to Yes: Negotiating Agreement Without Giving In* (New York: Penguin, 1991); William Ury, *Getting Past No: Negotiating Your Way from Confrontation to Cooperation* (New York: Bantam, 1993).

6 See Frank Fischer, *Citizens, Experts and the Environment: The Politics of Local Knowledge* (Durham and London: Duke University Press, 2000).

7 See Nicholas Dorochoff, *Negotiation Basics for Cultural Resource Managers* (Walnut Creek, CA: Left Coast Press, 2007).

8 Raymond Cohen, *Negotiating Across Cultures. International Communication in an Interdependent World,* 2nd ed. (Washington, DC: United States Institute of Peace, 2002).

9 See Deborah Tannen, *The Argument Culture. Stopping America's War of Words* (New York: Ballantine Books, 1999).

10 Dorochoff, *Negotiation Basics,* p. 16.

11 Fisher and Ury, *Getting to Yes,* p. 4.

12 Fischer, *Citizens,* p. xi.

13 Fischer, *Citizens,* p. 131.

14 See *http://www.africanburialground.gov/ABG_Main.htm.* I've also discussed the African Burial Ground and a mirror-image project in Philadelphia that was done right: see T.F. King, *Cultural Resource Laws and Practice,* 3rd ed. (Lanham, MD: AltaMira Press, 2008) , pp. 6–7, 81–82.

15 40 CFR 1501.6; 40 CFR 1508.5

16 36 CFR 800.3, especially 800.3(f).

17 36 CFR 800.2(c)(5).

18 36 CFR 800.3(f).

19 I can't refer directly to the case because of lawyer-client restrictions; I was an expert witness for one of the parties in a lawsuit.

20 See *http://www.achp.gov/book/case132.html;* the case is also discussed in King, *Cultural Resource Laws and Practice,* pp. 136–138, and *Places That Count: Traditional Cultural Properties in Cultural Resource Management* (Walnut Creek, CA: AltaMira Press, 2003), pp. 150–151.

21 If you're not federally recognized, you're not a tribe in the eyes of the law, however legitimate you may be historically. Tribal recognition and the lack thereof is a huge, complicated set of issues that I can't begin to do justice to. See Charles Wilkinson, *American Indians, Time, and the Law: Native Societies in a Modern Constitutional Democracy* (New Haven: Yale University Press, 1988).

22 The "trust" or "fiduciary" responsibility has been the subject of a great deal of litigation; again, Wilkinson is a good starting point for exploring the matter.

Chapter Seven

1 The late Helen F. King, to whose memory I mean no disrespect, but I never thought this rule made much sense.

2 40 CFR 1508.27.

3 40 CFR 1508.27(b)(4).

4   Issued by President Bill Clinton in 1995.

5   An appendix to the EA by BNSF engineer Robert J. Boileau documents that he actually read Dr. Nemati's report, in the course of preparing its out-of-hand rejection. What's lacking is any evidence that BLM or the Corps gave the report or Gordon Clark's rebuttal of Boileau's analysis any attention at all.

6   BNSF's tunnel alternative was 3,200 feet long, and the EA is unclear as to how it would be built, whether by tunneling or through some kind of cut-and-cover operation. Dr. Nemati's tunnel alternatives were 7,500 and 18,300 feet long, to be dug using state-of-the-art modern tunneling machines.

7   40 CFR 1508.27(b)(5).

8   BLM Manual H-3150—*Onshore Oil and Gas Geophysical Exploration Surface Management Requirements*.

9   A subsequent letter from BLM to the SHPO (8/7/2007) claimed that the geophysical standards didn't really apply (since BNSF was building a railroad, not doing geophysical exploration), but said that the monitoring program would begin at low particle velocities and work its way up.

Chapter Eight

1   Mr. Obama was responding to the question: "How would you balance energy development and recreational uses . . . with the management needs of wildlife that depend on Bureau of Land Management habitat?" in *Audubon Magazine* 110:5 (Sept.–Oct. 2008): 58–61. There's an unfortunate tendency among both politicians and environmentalists to treat NEPA and NHPA as though they were issues only for land management agencies, so no one ever asks the more general question: "What are you going to do about the wretched state of environmental impact assessment?" Mr. Obama's answer to the BLM question, however, suggests what his answer would be to the general EIA question if it were ever asked.

2   Lynton Keith Caldwell, *The National Environmental Policy Act: An Agenda for the Future* (Bloomington: Indiana University Press, 1998), p. 155.

3   Caldwell, *National Environmental Policy Act*, pp. 155–172.

4   Frank Fischer, *Citizens, Experts, and the Environment: The Politics of Local Knowledge* (Durham, NC: Duke University Press, 2000): see esp. chap. 1.

5   40 CFR 1501.7; 40 CFR 1503.1.

6   36 CFR 800.

7   Caldwell, *National Environmental Policy Act*, p. 157.

8   Caldwell, *National Environmental Policy Act*, p. 159.

9   See *http://www.ecr.gov/*, accessed September 1, 2008.

10 December 2007; see *http://ceq.hss.doe.gov/nepa/Citizens_Guide_Dec07.pdf*, accessed September 1, 2008.

11 CEQ *Citizen's Guide,* p. 6.

12 NEPA sec. 101(a).

13 NEPA sec. 101(b)(1).

14 NEPA sec. 101(b)(2).

15 NEPA sec. 101(b)(3).

[16] NEPA sec. 101(b)(4).

[17] NEPA sec. 101(b)(4).

[18] NEPA sec. 101(b)(5).

[19] NEPA sec. 101(b)(6).

[20] NEPA sec. 101(b)(6).

[21] NHPA, sec. 2.

[22] NHPA sec. 110(d).

[23] See, for example, *Lee v. Thornburgh*, 707 F. Supp. 600 (D.D.C. 03/1/1989); *Indiana Coal Council, Inc. v. Lujan*, 774 F. Supp. 1385 (D.D.C. 10/7/1991); *National Trust for Historic Preservation v. Blanck*, 938 F. Supp. 908 (D.D.C. 09/13/1996).

[24] Rubenson, Aroesty, and Thompsen, *Two Shades of Green, http://www.rand.org/pubs/reports/2007/R4220.pdf.*

[25] NEPA, Secs. 202, 204(3), 204(4).

[26] NEPA, Sec. 201; this responsibility is given to the president, and one is only left to assume that CEQ will be tasked to prepare the report (see also Sec. 204(7)).

[27] NEPA, Sec. 202.

[28] Caldwell, *National Environmental Policy Act*, p. 164.

[29] House Joint Resolution 33; see *http://www.opencongress.org/bill/110-hj33/show*, accessed September 3, 2008.

[30] Caldwell, *National Environmental Policy Act*, p. 163.

[31] Richard Marcinko, *Rogue Warrior* (New York: Simon and Schuster, 1992).

[32] NEPA, Sec. 102(C).

[33] 40 CFR 1508.14.

[34] 40 CFR 1508.27.

[35] 40 CFR 1501.3, 1508.9.

[36] 40 CFR 1502.24.

[37] NEPA, Sec. 102(C), last paragraph.

[38] 40 CFR 1501(a); this introductory paragraph is the only place in the regulations where section 101 is mentioned.

[39] Al Gore?

[40] Sharon Beder, "Bias and Credibility in Environmental Impact Assessment," *Chain Reaction* 68 (February 1993):28–30; *http://homepage.mac.com/herinst/sbeder/EIS.html* (accessed September 15, 2008). See also Sharon Beder, *Environmental Principles and Policies* (London: Earthscan, 2006). In "Bias and Credibility," Beder—whose work I just discovered—goes on to suggest many of the same changes I have. It's a bit embarrassing to find that she did so some fifteen years ago, but her proposals have obviously not yet taken hold, at least on this side of the Pacific.

Appendix

[1] Or sometimes *preliminary environmental impact statement*. There are many permutations on these terms—for example, *PSDEIS, preliminary supplemental draft environmental impact statement*.

Books by Tom King

Saving Places That Matter: A Citizen's Guide to the National Historic Preservation Act. Left Coast Press, 2007.

The Archaeological Survey Manual. With Greg White. Left Coast Press, 2006.

Doing Archaeology: A Cultural Resource Management Perspective. Left Coast Press, 2005.

Cultural Resource Laws and Practice: An Introductory Guide. AltaMira Press, 2008 (1st edition, 1998; 2nd edition, 2004).

Amelia Earhart's Shoes. With R. Jacobson, K. Burns, and K. Spading. AltaMira Press, 2004 (1st edition, 2001).

Places That Count: Traditional Cultural Properties in Cultural Resource Management. AltaMira Press, 2003.

Thinking about Cultural Resource Management: Essays from the Edge. AltaMira Press, 2002.

Federal Projects and Historic Places: The Section 106 Process. AltaMira Press, 2001.

Sources and Further Reading

SOME BOOKS ABOUT ENVIRONMENTAL IMPACT ASSESSMENT AND THE NATIONAL ENVIRONMENTAL POLICY ACT

Bass, R., A. Herson, and K. Bogdan
    2001   *The NEPA Book*. Solano Press, Point Arena, CA.
Caldwell, Lynton Keith
    1998   *The National Environmental Policy Act: An Agenda for the Future*. Indiana University Press, Bloomington, IN.
Canter, Larry W.
    1995   *Environmental Impact Assessment*. McGraw-Hill, New York.
Council on Environmental Quality
    1997   *The National Environmental Policy Act: A Study of Its Effectiveness after 25 Years*. Council on Environmental Quality, Washington, DC.
    2007   *A Citizen's Guide to the NEPA*. Council on Environmental Quality, Washington, DC.
Eccleston, Charles H.
    2000   *Environmental Impact Statements: A Comprehensive Guide to Project and Strategic Planning*. Wiley, New York.
    2008   *NEPA and Environmental Planning: Tools, Techniques, and Approaches for Practitioners*. CRC Press, Boca Raton, FL.
Environmental Law Institute
    1995   *Rediscovering the National Environmental Policy Act: Back to the Future*. Environmental Law Institute, New York.

Fischer, Frank
   2000   *Citizens, Experts, and the Environment: The Politics of Local Knowledge.* Duke University Press, Durham, NC.
Fogleman, Valerie
   1990   *Guide to the National Environmental Policy Act: Interpretations, Applications, and Compliance.* Quorum, New York.
Hildebrand, Stephen G.
   1993   *Environmental Analysis: The NEPA Experience.* CRC, Boca Raton, FL.
Lindstrom, Matthew J., and Zachary A. Smith
   2001   *The National Environmental Policy Act: Judicial Misconstruction, Legislative Indifference, and Executive Neglect.* Texas A&M University Press, College Station, TX.
Noble, Bram F.
   2005   *Introduction to Environmental Impact Assessment: A Guide to Principles and Practice.* Oxford University Press, New York.
Rubenson, David, Jerry Aroesty, and Charles Thompsen
   1991   *Two Shades of Green: Environmental Protection and Combat Training.* Rand Arroyo Center, Los Angeles.

SOME BOOKS ABOUT CULTURAL RESOURCE MANAGEMENT AND THE NATIONAL HISTORIC PRESERVATION ACT

Advisory Council on Historic Preservation
   2002   *Protecting Historic Properties: A Citizen's Guide to Section 106 Review.* Advisory Council on Historic Preservation, Washington, DC.
Dorochoff, Nicholas,
   2007   *Negotiation Basics for Cultural Resource Managers.* Left Coast Press, Walnut Creek, CA.
King, T. F.
   2007   *Saving Places That Matter: A Citizen's Guide to the National Historic Preservation Act.* Left Coast Press, Walnut Creek, CA.
   2008   *Cultural Resource Laws and Practice.* 3rd web site. AltaMira Press, Lanham, MD.

OTHER SOURCES CITED

Beder, Sharon
    2006   *Environmental Principles and Policies.* Earthscan, London

Cohen, Raymond,
    2002   *Negotiating across Cultures. International Communication in an Interdependent World.* 2nd edition. United States Institute of Peace, Washington, DC.

Fischer, Frank
    2000   *Citizens, Experts and the Environment: The Politics of Local Knowledge.* Duke University Press, Durham and London.

Fisher, Roger, and William Ury
    1991   *Getting to Yes: Negotiating Agreement without Giving In.* Penguin, New York.

King, T. F.
    2003   *Places That Count: Traditional Cultural Properties in Cultural Resource Management.* AltaMira Press, Walnut Creek, CA.

Marcinko, Richard
    1992   *Rogue Warrior.* Simon and Schuster, New York.

Nadeem, Obaidullah and Riizwan Hameed
    2008   Evaluation of Environmental Impact Assessment System in Pakistan. *Environmental Impact Assessment Review* 28/8: 562–571. Elsevier, Amsterdam.

Tannen, Deborah
    1999   *The Argument Culture. Stopping America's War of Words.* Ballantine books, New York.

Ury, William
    1993   *Getting Past No: Negotiating Your Way from Confrontation to Cooperation.* Bantam, New York.

Wilkinson, Charles
    1988   *American Indians, Time, and the Law: Native Societies in a Modern Constitutional Democracy.* Yale University Press, New Haven, CT.

Index

About the Author

Thomas F. (Tom) King has worked in and around environmental impact assessment (EIA) and cultural resource management (CRM) since the 1960s. He holds a Ph.D. in anthropology, and has carried out archaeological fieldwork in California and Micronesia, but by the early 1970s he had come to focus on EIA and what was to become known as CRM. Over the years he has worked as a private consultant, as an academic researcher, and in government for the Advisory Council on Historic Preservation, the General Services Administration, the National Park Service, and the (now disbanded) government of the Trust Territory of the Pacific Islands. He is the author of seven textbooks on aspects of cultural resource management, together with scores of journal articles and government guidelines, regulations, and other publications. He has served as an expert witness in litigation under the National Environmental Policy Act (NEPA) and the National Historic Preservation Act (NHPA), helped draft comprehensive amendments to NHPA in 1992, and oversaw development of the General Service Administration's NEPA procedures in the late 1990s. Today he works as a private consultant and trainer, associated with SWCA Environmental Consultants (which has had no role in producing this book, and does not necessarily subscribe to anything in it). He also serves as Senior Archaeologist on The International Group for Historic Aircraft Recovery's (TIGHAR) Amelia Earhart Project, and is the co-author of a 2004 book, *Amelia Earhart's Shoes,* describing the research and TIGHAR's adventures seeking the lost aviation pioneer in the South Pacific. King can be contacted by email at *tfking106@aol.com*, and blogs at *http://crmplus.blogspot.com/*.